gardens in perspective

gardens
in perspective
jerry harpur

*For Marjorie, our sons Nicholas,
Robert, Marcus, and Daniel, and
their families, with love*

First published in the United Kingdom
by Mitchell Beazley
The Octopus Publishing Group

Text copyright © Jerry Harpur 2005
Photographs copyright © Jerry Harpur
Design and layout © Mitchell Beazley 2005

British Library Cataloguing in Publication Data
A CIP catalogue record for this book is
available from the British Library

ISBN 1 84000 771 0

Commissioning editor: Michèle Byam
Executive art editor: Sarah Rock
Design: Ken Wilson
Editor: Joanna Chisholm
Index: Sue Farr
Production: Gary Hayes

Typeset in Gothic

Printed and bound in China by

Toppan Printing Company Limited

Prelims pictures
Half title: Garden in Belgium/designed by
Jacques Wirtz, Schoten
Title page: Rashtrapati Bhavan Garden at
the President's Palace, New Delhi, India
Contents page: Desert garden, Tucson,
Arizona, USA/designed by Steve Martino

contents

foreword
penelope hobhouse

In recent years garden photography has reached a peak of perfection in which, as an art form, it measures up to achievements of the greatest landscape painters. As a discipline it requires a knowledge and skill in technique, and an understanding of the changing forms of light and shade and how colours alter and affect each other. As a record of gardens it far outshines any possible written descriptions and, until quite recently with the coming of digital, it cannot "lie". What you see is what is there. But the photographer can add a further dimension. By capturing a moment of time in the garden, be it at dawn with the early sun's rays or as light fades at twilight, his or her fleeting snapshot reveals the effects of atmospheric conditions on how you see it. Like an impressionist painting, frozen on canvas, the picture chosen by the photographer portrays an "ideal" instant. Today, great garden photographers such as Jerry Harpur are inspired and influenced by the great Impressionists – and especially Claude Monet, who planted his riots of colour in his garden at Giverny in order later to portray them in his paintings – but in the last years of the 19th century the painters themselves were encouraged by contemporary developments in photography to see their art as capturing similar single moments frozen on canvas, using primary colours and portraying shadows as reflections of light. It is clear to a photographer such as Jerry that gardeners are equally influenced by the Impressionist painters, their design vision coloured not by one static vista but by a series of unfolding garden views. It is the photographer's task to understand the designer's purpose and to make a modern landscape more real to the casual viewer. By choosing to portray one picture he or she can convey the whole spirit of the garden.

In *Gardens in Perspective* Jerry Harpur plays a dual role. His beautiful pictures, which embrace old and new landscapes, are accompanied by his own text, in which he describes not only what you see but the ideas behind the garden concept. To do this he has had, not only to travel the globe, but to devote many hours to talking to modern designers in order to understand the essentials of their art. The book is divided into appropriate chapters which cover themes rather than any chronological order, tracing influences through the centuries and opening readers' eyes to cultural effects which take traditional styles and develop them anew in different and often exotic settings. The book also gives the reader a chance to understand Harpur's own interests and preferences. With his photographer's eye and with a vast experience of working in different lights and in climates allowing an inexhaustible range of plant material, he conveys his own excitement. His pictures of modern gardens reveal his love of new architectural schemes involving considerable engineering skills. Above all he sees gardens as an art form and has devoted much of his life to interpreting garden beauty. We are all fortunate to have *Gardens in Perspective* as our guide book to the appreciation of garden landscape and as a celebration of Jerry Harpur's work.

The distinguished writer, garden designer, and historian Penelope Hobhouse created her third garden around an old coach house at Bettiscombe, Dorset, UK. The gravel garden contains perennials such as tall lupins (*Lupinus arboreus*) and *Phlomis russeliana*, as well as the grass *Stipa gigantea*, which glows golden in the afternoon sun. Nearer the stone pool is purple-flowered sage (*Salvia transsylvanica*).

Gardening was the first creative thing I did as a child, and I little expected that aspects of it would become so compulsive. Socially it is a great leveller, a meritocracy where, if talent and hard work are combined to maximum effect, acceptance is not hard to come by. I had a talented grandmother called Charlotte Harpur, whose wisdom I relished quite early, when I was eight and she 70. I already enjoyed the delights of her garden at Burton Latimer Hall in Northamptonshire, UK, when I began to realize that the garden was becoming the main focus of my visits. Later on, I discovered that I had inherited her interest in photography. This was triggered by the discovery of a second-hand Brownie box camera in a chemist's shop when I was 13. From then onwards, I had tunnel vision about landscape photography. The first black-and-white print I made was of the long double border in my grandmother's garden. I didn't know until later that she had been a pioneering amateur photographer, producing half-plate glass negatives of antiques, and that she wrote and photographed for the magazine *Country Life* – as do I and my son Marcus.

Only years later was I able to combine professionally my two great interests – photography and gardens. As this was at the beginning of the gardening boom in the early

In September 1992, John Brookes introduced me to Keith Kirsten, South Africa's best-known gardener, who ensured that I discovered his country's gardens. One early morning in the Nyanga township near Cape Town, I was introduced to Rob Small, who runs the Abalimi Bezekhaya Nyanga plant nursery for the benefit of the township. One of the most delightful township gardens was cared for by Stanford Sobambela, whose front garden was bright with ranunculus flowers – and his cheerful smile (*bottom centre*). Rob and I (*bottom left*) were

introduction
jerry harpur

surrounded by not only children and footballers but also soldiers on guard – this being before Nelson Mandela came to power.

The generally harsh light in South Africa is very different from that found at Giverny, in Normandy, France, where Claude Monet reproduced the light so sensitively in his paintings. The atmosphere of the Giverny garden is one of the most inspirational anywhere. Fortunately, most of my visits, as here on an early summer morning with poppies and roses catching the light (*below*), have been in good conditions.

1980s, it was comparatively easy for me to stop my work for advertising agencies. Realizing that the American book-buying public would soon tire of reading British-produced books on garden design unless they included more pictures of American gardens, in 1983 I flew to Charleston, South Carolina. For 16 days, I photographed as many gardens as I could find, driving up the east coast of the USA to Long Island. In this way, I began an affair, still going on, with America and its gardens. Much of the best and most exciting garden design is happening there, particularly on the west coast.

My photography of gardens has been influenced by the paintings of Claude Monet more than anything else. His painted series of the haystacks at Giverny, Normandy, France, demonstrate the variety of directions and colours of sunlight from dawn to dusk and in different seasons. With no formal art training, this was something I had not fully appreciated until I was well into photographing gardens. Monet's garden at Giverny is one of the most delightful to be in, especially early in the morning and late in the evening, a privilege which photographers are sometimes allowed. This was, of course, Monet's own favourite way of using the light. So much photography depends on luck: it could be said

that conditions are only perfect twice a year, when the light is doing just what you want it to do. A painter can help that, putting his or her own brush strokes in later. This can now be said of the digital photographer, too.

Of all the arts, gardening is surely the most ephemeral. Gardens grow, they are never the same from year to year, and owners change. Even if the garden has no plants (depending only on design paint and materials), the weather and the atmosphere guarantee deterioration. This all affects the way that I take photographs of a garden.

On arrival in a garden, I assess its character and how and when it should be photographed, although I usually have a fair idea already. If I go to Arizona, USA, to see the designer Steve Martino, I am confident of excellent Minimalist structure, desert plants, and colour. However, in Sydney, Australia, I have no idea what to expect, because Vladimir Sitta works out his ideas at the drawing board, where he is often inspired by history, the elements, and the more dramatic arts.

Garden photography poses a unique challenge when compared with other types of photography. A photographer needs to learn about modern design as well as about

The last 20 years in gardening
have been extremely exciting
both in design and in new plant
propagation, all over the world.
Cottage gardens, for example,
have taken on a new look.
Having restored his thatched
cottage near Bury St Edmunds,
Suffolk, UK, Jorn Langberg then
asked Paul Miles to design a
herb garden surrounded by yew
hedges (*left*). Beside them, he
planted grey-leaved *Pyrus
salicifolia* (successfully clipped
into a dome shape), hawthorn,
sumach, and holly, which are
especially colourful in autumn.

   While Langberg's garden
contains fairly traditional
planting and design, a totally
different kind of garden design is
this one by Topher Delaney (*right*),
a conceptual artist who uses few
plants and is very strong on
hardscaping and structure. Her
roof-top garden in San Francisco,
USA, contains different shapes
and tones of blue materials in
furniture and flooring, with small
palms in dark blue containers.
The space is purely functional as
a living area, with a large dark
blue-covered bed in a corner.
How much more different could
two gardens be than these?

advancing digital technology, which has many post-shoot advantages for producing the perfect image. It also helps to know something about the ways of living plants, even if only to gauge when they will be at their best. Other skills needed when photographing gardens vary, but two of the most important ones are a sense of composition and the ability to use light, recording the prevailing conditions. The light can be good before sunrise, with the help of a yellow filter to soften the amount of blue sky reflected in places the sun has yet to reach. There is also less breeze at that time to blur long exposures. Night photography, of artificial lighting, is best done at dusk, in the ten minutes when the fading light still balances the artificially lit areas.

As with the great Impressionists such as Monet, the rendering of the true atmosphere is the ideal, but it often means photographing very early in the morning or late in the evening. It can be especially challenging to produce dramatic or atmospheric photographs in poor weather, but the results can be truly memorable at times, such as as in my images of gardens at Nooroo (*see p.71*), Beirut (*see p.112*), and Manor House (*see p.178*).

A further challenge for someone like myself, who is not a garden historian, is putting modern designs into perspective with work that was done in the time of the Italian Renaissance, or in the 18th century by the great André Le Nôtre and William Kent. Once I have understood the background to such gardens, I feel better able to interpet them for other people.

During the course of my work, I have been extraordinarily fortunate to meet someone like the owner of Le Nôtre's Vaux le Vicomte, near Paris, France. Count Patrice de Vogue tells me that he was given Vaux le Vicomte as a wedding present – but without the means to maintain it. Yet here was Le Nôtre's first great masterpiece (more intimate than Versailles), which influenced the way in which at least three key modern designers (Dan Kiley, Martha Schwartz, and Tom Stuart-Smith) use large spaces. Kiley, from Vermont, USA, had been particularly inspired after his travels in 1945 around western Europe, where for the first time in his life he experienced "formal, spatial built landscapes (as championed in France by Le Nôtre, at its grandest, most rarefied level, yet found on

In spring, the Great Dixter daffodil meadow at Northiam, East Sussex, UK, flows from the house towards the Sussex Downs (*top left*). One summer morning, in Dixter's tropical garden, Christopher Lloyd's voice called "Is Jerry there?" and he appeared from behind red cannas, closely followed by Beth Chatto – the first time I had seen the friends together. Beth picked Japanese anemone flowers to complete a portrait (*top right*) of two people whose love of plants has been a case of spontaneous combustion, setting fires of enthusiasm among gardeners of all ages. By contrast, Carol Valentine's stunning garden (*right*) in Montecito, California, USA, designed by Isabelle C. Greene, is a contemporary garden of exotic plants. A "pool" of polished slate is encircled by triangles of brown berry (*Sedum rubrotintum*), overlooked by green and grey agaves (*A. attenuata and A. parryi*).

every street of tiny towns and cities)". Roberto Burle Marx, the very influential 20th-century, Brazilian garden designer, was also a keen traveller and gleaned many of his ideas from Europe, especially Germany. Fernando Caruncho, the great Spanish landscape architect, spent a lot of time in Africa, as did Luis Barragán. The originality and beauty of many of Barragán's designs, including the Tlalpan Convent in Mexico City, are renowned for their mastery of space and use of single-colour walls. The latter style has been adopted by various present-day garden designers.

I am always fascinated by the way international garden design has developed and by the surprises that have turned up recently. Shunmyo Masuno is a Zen priest in Japan of enviable intellect and achievement, who is working for international projects as well as great hotels and museums in Japan. He also lectures all over the world. Another exciting designer, Vladimir Djurovic (half Slovak, half Lebanese), caused a sensation in London in spring 2005, when projecting his expensive Minimalist work for the Society of Garden Designers.

Also, towards the end of the 20th century, a new interpretation of formality in garden design emerged, just when it might have been thought predictable. This is exemplified

Another good, long-time friend was Rosemary Verey, who I photographed (*top left*) on the day of her return from a three-week lecture tour, zigzagging around America. She remarked that this was not the ideal day to do a portrait, but she was so delighted to be back in her garden that she'd do anything. The setting was her conservatory at Barnsley House, in Gloucestershire, UK, with Simon Verity's grotto in the background, styled by herself. Verey also framed the potager at The Old Rectory, Sudborough, UK, with the climbing rose 'Rambling Rector' (*top centre*).

John Brookes is a garden designer I have long admired. He introduced me to South Africa and Argentina, and encouraged me to go there to meet Roberto Burle Marx, which to my regret I failed to do. John is one of the best informed and most widely influential of the present-day, established designers, and his lectures on the relationship of garden design to the landscape are a revelation. John's garden at Fontwell, Sussex, UK, ranges from a walled gravel garden to the naturalistic, as seen here in a view taken by the pool (*bottom left*).

most of all by Belgium's Jacques Wirtz and his son Peter, whose work also appears in Paris (Jardins des Tuileries), Moscow, and Switzerland. Their classically shaped hedges, arbours, and parterres are designed within the garden's contours and remain unique.

I too have travelled extensively in the course of my work, and this book is a travelling garden photographer's impression of the last 20 years all over the world. It does not seek to be an exhaustive book of great garden design. Many of the best-known gardens and garden designers are here, and so too are many gems that are not open to the general public. The "Perspective" of the title is intended not only to define where earlier inspirations for modern designers come from but also to give an opportunity for the art of gardening to be illustrated as the creative force that it has been for so long.

Gardens in Perspective has been an inspirational book to put together, not least because of the designers and garden owners whose gardens are here. Many have become my friends. Their personalities are as diverse as the gardens, and it has been an interesting exercise deciding on the chapter themes most appropriate to the variety of design styles and plants all over the world. Some of their themes reflect traditional concepts of garden design, such as formal gardens and Minimalism, while others have a more subjective slant, such as fantasy & romance, and naturalism. The latter reflect how I perceive the gardens; others might well not agree with my choice.

Some gardens would have been suitable for more than one chapter, and parts of several gardens appear in more than one chapter when they are relevant to more than one theme. Thus Sitta's work appears in three different chapters: "Sensuous minimalism", "The exotic look", and "The garden as art".

Our own garden is dominated by plants, and this may explain why I have included a chapter called "A passion for plants". It is filled with places I have visited that have been created by legendary plantsmen and women such as Christopher Lloyd and Beth Chatto, as well as by non-professional enthusiasts, who love the garden world and happen to be excellent gardeners. Another chapter, "The new naturalism", covers gardens where living plants provide enormous satisfaction when they actually do as the designer intended, while "The exotic look" chapter includes a wide range of unusual plantings, from Roberto Burle Marx's designs to the English annual flowers in New Delhi, India.

Because of the ever-changing nature of plants, the chapter on contemporary formality was one of the most appropriate to illustrate the succession of ideas where recent thinkers such as Rosemary Verey, Julian and Isabel Bannerman, and Ulf Nordfjell have often used formal settings to express planting ideas. "Fantasy & romance" is about gardens that gave me unexpected pleasure – not because they conformed to a particular style but because they inspired some kind of emotive reaction, as at Innisfree, in upstate New York, USA, or Nindooinbah in Queensland, Australia. The equally eclectic "The garden as art" chapter is pure self-indulgence, which I hope the reader will enjoy as much as I have had pleasure in selecting the photographs to go in it, while in "Sensuous minimalism" I have included both Steve Martino and Vladimir Sitta, who are highly successful artists, from different directions. I am thrilled by the modern approach to Minimalism, with some of its roots in the work of Thomas Church and Luis Barragan, and very much wonder "what's next?"

I hope that you too will be inspired by the gardens illustrated in *Gardens in Perspective* and will want to imitate some of the designs. However, gardens themselves should also be visited, where possible. There is nothing quite like the beauty of the real thing.

Classical formal design began with the Italian Renaissance, which was at its height during the 15th and 16th centuries, spreading into 17th- and 18th-century Persia and France. British designers such as William Kent began to realize this dream in the 18th-century English Landscape Movement, which freed gardens from strict formality and introduced romanticism, as at Stowe in Buckinghamshire.

Formalism has been reinterpreted by many contemporary landscape and garden designers, including Penelope Hobhouse, who contends that there is life after the very influential, early 20th-century garden designer Gertrude Jekyll, after all. Hobhouse wrote that, "it is remarkable how much of the work of modern designers such as Russell Page, Sir Geoffrey Jellicoe, Thomas Church, Fernando Caruncho, and Jacques Wirtz contains references to the Renaissance period". Indeed, her own garden pays tribute to both traditional and contemporary formality.

Some seemingly traditional formal gardens are, however, a mixture of original and relatively recent planting. Others can only be loosely termed formal, their design being a recent interpretation of this style.

contemporary formality

Previous pages: The Music Garden at Château Villandry, in France, was planted only in 1912, although its canals and terraces were created in the 18th century.

It was during the Renaissance that gardens began to be perceived as sophisticated living areas, often reflecting the landscape around them. They were another form of artistic expression, mostly classical and structural, and so were unlike anything that had gone before.
Bottom left: The present garden of the 9th-century Castello di Vignanello near Rome, Italy, was designed and planted at the end of the Renaissance, in 1603. It remains in its original form, mainly because it has been owned by the same family – the Ruspolis – ever since then.
Bottom right: The Renaissance influence spread to France where, over half a century later, the Château de Vaux le Vicomte was built near Paris, France, by Nicholas Fouquet, King Louis XIV's finance minister. Fouquet inspired the previously untried André Le Nôtre to create several levels of parterres, canals, and fountains along an axis of 3.5km (2 miles). This brilliantly designed garden aroused the jealousy of the king, who arrested Fouquet and hired Le Nôtre to build him a garden at his palace in Versailles, also outside Paris. Le Nôtre's use of space greatly influenced contemporary formal designers such as Dan Kiley, Martha Schwartz (*see pp.250–3*), and Tom Stuart-Smith (*see p.56*).
Top right: By the 1730s, William Kent was creating landscape gardens in England at Rousham Park, Oxfordshire, and at Stowe (*see p.238*). The former is linked by walks, streams, and rills. Its seven-arched portico Praeneste is not only one of the most beautiful features in the garden but it also affords a view over the surrounding countryside – a forerunner of our own love of borrowed landscape.

The formal gardens of ancient Persia began to be created 2,500 years ago as part of the spiritual culture of Muslim society.

Above: Formality *par excellence* is evident at the 2.6ha (6½ acre) Bagh-e Fin garden, Kashan. It was probably designed by Shah 'Abbas I in the 16th century, and it comprises a vast geometric pattern of squares and rectangles. In the middle of the garden are a pavilion and square pool surrounded by a network of rills, paths, and 400-year-old cypresses. All the rills have gravity-operated, bubbling jets of water arising from blue cones set at regular intervals. At times, as here, the rills flow around square pools of still water.

Right: Although softened a great deal by the planting, the Persian tradition of formality and water was carried on by the Shah of Persia. In the 1930s, he built Bagh-e Moustoufi with a walled garden in the countryside outside Tehran. Farthest away from the house is a large pool surrounded by pots of aspidistra. It is fed by water from the mountains and is connected to an octagonal fountain via a rill.

Water flowing in rills occurs in all four of these gardens.
Left: For Sir William Walton's 80th birthday, his friend Russell Page designed a long rill for La Mortella, his island home on Ischia, Italy. Here the sound of water combines with birdsong among rich plantings of elephant-eared alocasias and in a Moorish-inspired pool.
Top right: A stone staircase, with water rills cut into either side of the steps, is Sir Terence Conran's method of joining three levels visually. These were created in order to mitigate the effects of the Mistral in his garden in Provence, France, which slopes downwards, towards the villa.
Bottom centre: The *canaleta* was a favourite garden feature used by the Moors (as at the Alhambra), and Fernando Caruncho has used the device in the Camp S'Arch garden, Menorca, Spain. Here it follows a bend in the stone path towards the house.
Bottom right: Steve Martino's rill for a client in Tucson, Arizona, USA, is as much a practical retaining wall to stop the desert falling on to the front drive as it is an attractive feature to greet visitors on their arrival.

These two formal gardens, created from detailed research but with different interpretations, reflect styles of formality nearly 400 years apart.

Above: Around the time that the garden at Castello di Vignanello was created, Sir Robert Cecil built Hatfield House, in Hertfordshire, UK, a great Jacobean masterpiece. John Tradescant the Elder designed the formal gardens, but they fell into disrepair, so in 1972 the then Lady Salisbury began to recreate the feel of a Jacobean garden.

My joy of anticipation while driving to Hatfield through hoar frost-encrusted avenues on a mid-winter morning was realized when David Beaumont, the head gardener, took me on to the roof of the house. From there we could view the two avenues of holm oaks (*Quercus ilex*) sculpted into perfect lollipops and lining either side of the parterre beds. Beyond, the 19th-century maze (*right*) glistened four-square in front of the New Pond, a lake dug 400 years ago.

Far right: Reflections in the still pools at Camp S'Arch on the Spanish island of Menorca reminded me of the formal gardens of Persia. Fernando Caruncho, the landscape architect and philosopher, has built 16 pools here, five of which are on an axis with the pavilion with its vine-clad window grilles. This, in itself, repeats the grid pattern of the pools, which are set within tightly clipped squares of *escallonia* and separated by stone paths.

When they redesigned Houghton Hall in Norfolk, UK, Julian and Isabel Bannerman drew a great deal on history, be it Arab gardens, the world of antiquity, or the formal gardens of Europe before the 18th century. They were fascinated by the lost world of English formal gardens full of architecture, terraces, and *objets d'art.* "Impossible to do now", sighed Isabel Bannerman, "too expensive, so we are always striving to produce gardens that are of our time".

The Bannermans referred to André Le Nôtre's work in France, when designing the pleached limes (*top left*) in the walled garden. This provides a simple contrast with the riotous borders elsewhere at Houghton Hall. The oak obelisks act as a portal to this garden, and the stone obelisk collected by Houghton Hall's owner, Lord Cholmondeley, makes the focal point in the gravel between strips of mown grass.

In late spring the cherry walk (*bottom left*) blooms for several days with magnificent dark and light blue flag irises.

A typical Bannerman touch is the Temple (*right*) at the end of the 120m (400ft) long borders. The pediment there is filled with antlers from the deer in the park.

The formality of the Italian Renaissance and the perspectives of French 18th-century gardens have been adapted to the flat landscape of Le Jardin Plume, Patrick and Sylvie Quibel's barn garden in Normandy, France.

Structure within the garden is formed by the plants themselves with hedges of hornbeam, box, and beech. Within this boxwood parterre (*top left*) flourish the red *Crocosmia* 'Lucifer', yellow stars of *Asphodeline liburnica*, and the copper-red *Helenium* 'Moerheim Beauty' along with dahlias and day lilies. In the early morning mist of late summer, cattle graze in the field beyond.

The Quibels' potager (*bottom left*) is bounded, palisade-like, by a willow fence. Within criss-crossing brick paths, square beds lined with lavenders such as *Lavandula angustifolia* 'Hidcote' (purple) and *L.a*. 'Jean Davis' (pale pink) provide vegetables such as the unusual Saint-Saens cabbage.

In the red border, nasturtium flowers (*Tropaeolum majus*) surround the poppy *Papaver orientale* 'Lady Bird' (*bottom centre*) with stems of Japanese blood grass (*Imperata cylindrica* 'Rubra') colouring up on the left.

The mown paths through pink grass *Agrostis tenuis* in the apple orchard at Le Jardin Plume (*right*) were inspired by Great Dixter, in Sussex, UK (*see pp.80–1*).

The inspiration for this four-storey *pigeonnier* (*left*) and its gardens came from the 18th-century Pin Mill at Bodnant, in north Wales, and the Taj Mahal, India – an unlikely pair until you realize that both are reflected in long, formal stretches of water. Neither building, however, would have been appropriate to rural Quebec where this garden, Les Quatre Vents, is situated, so the owner, Frank Cabot, found a suitable compromise design in a 1926 book called *Small French Buildings*. In it, a photograph of a farm pigeon house in Gourdon satisfied one of Cabot's most tantalizing ambitions.

Frank Cabot is an American descendant of the 15th-century adventurer John Cabot. He is no less a pusher of boundaries, having created the Stone Crop garden in New York State, USA, and founded The Garden Conservancy, at Cold Spring, New York. Cabot also spent more than 20 years adding gardens of exotic origin to Les Quatre Vents, his family estate in Canada.

The work of two contemporary architects with an interest in formal garden design in the first half of the 20th century shared an admirer, Gertrude Jekyll, although it was only one, Sir Edwin Lutyens, who for 17 years worked with her.

Below: Their most successful collaboration was at Hestercombe in Somerset, UK, before World War I. Stone walls (*left*) and steps (some of them arranged in semi-circular flights) surround the main part of the formal garden, creating terraces at different levels. Rills in the same, buff-coloured stone, interspersed with circular stone loops, are set in immaculate lawns either side. Jekyll's ideas for soft-coloured plant associations are sensitively preserved at Hestercombe in both the triangular flower beds in the lower area of the garden known as The Plat, and in the long side borders.

Right: Harold Peto's architectural talents were mainly classical, based on Renaissance Italy. It is surprising therefore that Jekyll, then expounding the joys of natural gardening, should have been so keen on his Ionic-columnar style as to include various Peto designs in her book *Garden Ornament.* Peto's placement of his finds was masterly, as in this view at the entrance to his garden at Iford Manor, Wiltshire, UK.

In the years following the Renaissance, the landscape around Florence was covered with villas and gardens, of which the Villa Gamberaia, at Settignano, Italy, eventually became the best known. Its influence is also evident in the two other gardens shown here.
Below: At Villa Gamberaia, eight different areas are unified by a long grass allee, from end to end, as designed at the turn of the 19th century by head gardener Martino, father of the great designer Pietro Porcinai.

Columns of junipers are set in box parterres, which line four separate, formal pools. Roses and perennials bring spots of colour to the garden but, earlier, pink peonies add softer colours.

Right: Silvano, the head gardener at Gamberaia in the 1980s, advised the Florentine footballer Luciano Giubbilei about becoming a garden designer. Giubbilei is influenced by the classical order and geometric proportion of the Italian Renaissance and 17th-century France, and so has developed a clean, pure line in his formal gardens. He also loves softly shaped trees, such as *Carpinus betula*, as in this garden in north London, UK.
Far right: Giubbilei's roof garden in Kensington, London, UK, is as much a decoration to be seen from the conservatory, with its box balls and maples in French oak planters, as it is an outside living room.

Contemporary formal gardens can be entirely original or they can be derivative. They can use single plants in great drifts, mounds, and sweeps or in association with each other, or none at all, still within a framework of strong design. *Top left:* Peter Wirtz's garden design for the Ernsting Family factory near Cologne, Germany, has gone for simplicity of form and planting – and water – in a campus of architecture designed by David Chipperfield. Wirtz's variously shaped pools are bound together by the landscape design. Here is a composition of curving mounds of one kind of grass (*Pennisetum orientale*) with mown lawn and serpentine pathways that flow around and between the buildings (*bottom left*). It is so simple that the occasional tree (such as *Amelanchier laevis*, orange-leaved in the autumn light) suggests a selective arboretum. *Right:* Shunmyo Masuno, too, combined simplicity of form when he designed Zen gardens on three different levels at the Kojimachi Hotel in Tokyo, Japan. On one level he replaced the traditional *tokonoma*, which in a Japanese tea room is an alcove that contains a beautiful object, such as a scroll painting, to be admired. The *tokonama* he introduced took the form of a long pool and waterfalls outside a window. The water cascades over two kinds of stone: brown granite at the bottom of the wall supports many layers of black South Africa granite. These are chiselled at the edges to encourage the water into a controlled storm.

On possibly the steepest slope of any garden I know, this formal garden on the outskirts of Johannesburg, in South Africa, has gone through various evolutions in well over a century since the Boers built its narrow stone-walled terraces.

Gary Searle – the man with the vision to bring this garden back to life – was inspired by the grand hillside garden of La Casella in the south of France. He is not a professional gardener but is creative in the world of international design – hence the controlled way in which the garden has been restored and planted. It took three years, with the strongest feature emerging to be the long stone staircase (*bottom left*), rising from an axis which begins at the outside gate and runs up to a grotto half-covered by hanging plants and decorated by a 1930s' Jekyll pot. A few steps farther on and you reach the house. There are still more levels before the top gate is finally reached.

The terrace views are stunning, with lavender and Iceland poppies softening the walls (*top left*) and box balls in pots sitting atop the wall buttresses between style-defining Italian cypresses. A vista towards the city is interrupted by healthy-looking banana leaves and jacaranda blossom (*top centre*). Best of all, though, is the view down on to what I think is a thatched stone dovecote (good English idea, that), surrounded by a jacaranda tree (*right*), but Searle assures me that it is the garden shed.

André Le Nôtre's style is evident in the lowest of three tiers of terracing at Château Villandry in the Loire valley, in France. The box parterre known as The Music Garden (*see p.17*) overlooks the famous potager created by Dr Joachim Carvallo, great-grandfather of the present owner, nearly 100 years ago, in 1910. He was inspired by geometric patterns in engravings of 16th-century gardens by Androuet du Cerceau.

The potager consists of nine large squares, which, for much of the year, are brimming with colour and texture-contrasted plantings of vegetables (*top left*). Various standard roses and young pear trees (St Victor variety) rise above them at intervals within a pattern of clipped low boxwood.

In the centre of the potager, a formal arrangement of 16 rose-covered arbours helps the garden to look as if somebody lives here – the tower of the family home rising above it. Below, spikey cardoons and the purple leaves and white flower spikes of *Perilla frutescens* var. *nankinensis* catch the early light alongside the white cabbages.

Nearby the sun glances across mass plantings of purple decorative cabbages, *Brassica olearacea* (*below*); dark-leaved aubergines are still in shadow behind, with celery to the left. Most brilliant of all, though, is a bed of 'Gion Red' pimentos (*right*), which takes up the foreground, with frilly white cabbages, white beet leaves, and more perillas beyond. This is surely the most influential, stylistic vegetable garden of modern times.

Potagers form an integral part of many formal gardens, whether traditional or contemporary. *Right:* Two months before she died Rosemary Verey and I had lunch together at Barnsley House, in Gloucestershire, UK, and most of the food had come from her potager. Here was, arguably, the most appreciated part of her extraordinary garden, made all the more so because it derived its inspiration from two books by the 17th-century horticulturist the Revd William Lawson, as well as from the

potager at Château Villandry. Lawson wrote that housewives should have two gardens, one for flowers and one for vegetables; the flower garden may have herbs, and the vegetable garden could include a comely border. Thus, in mid-summer, Verey was growing strawberries and cabbages either side of a box-edged brick path in the same garden as red poppies, an arbour covered with the golden hop *Humulus lupulus,* potatoes, and the tall silver spikes of *Onopordum acanthium.*

Top right: Gwen and Don Davey, in Victoria, Australia, in turn, got the idea for their potager from Barnsley House. Later, they built a shade house so that Gwen Davey could propagate in the intense heat. Considering this was mid-summer, when the flower gardens were dry, the tomatoes, lettuces, spinach, and onions were remarkably fresh. *Top centre:* An idea for a *potager nomade* appeared at the Chaumont garden festival in France, in 1999. It was designed by Patrick Nadeau and might be

suitable for a small roof-top. The four sides unfold from a box so that on one side is a greenhouse, in the foreground a potager with furrows for watering, behind two rows of tomatoes, and to the right a rest platform. *Above:* Depending on how keen you are on gourds or on pure living artistry, Xa Tollemache's gourd tunnel at Helmingham, in Suffolk, UK, is, as Verey herself remarked, like stepping into the White Rabbit's tunnel in *Alice in Wonderland.* It ends in a seat bearing the family crest.

The formal foundations of Norrviken, at Bastad in southern Sweden, were laid by its owner Rudolf Abelin in 1906, so that there could be an interplay between a formal garden and the countryside. In 2002 Ulf Nordfjell was commissioned to develop the gardens, and later that year Tage Andersen, the Danish flower arranger and decorator, held an exhibition at Norrviken. In the Baroque garden, Andersen placed balls of clipped bay trees (*Laurus nobilis*) to line up in rows of three either side of the long pool, parallel with cut boxwood hedges, leading to the house (*above*). He softened the look with pink sidalcea, commonly known as prairie mallow. In the Renaissance garden, Andersen placed an iron basket in the middle of the red stone parterres with white-flowered *Solanum laxum* growing through (*below*).

Farther down the garden, Nordfjell then planted hedges of white *Gaura lindheimeri* 'Whirling Butterflies' in front of the long carpinus ones.

After that, the transition to the countryside began, when Nordfjell planted meadow-like annuals into strict formal beds. He emphasized the countryside by using just one genus, verbena, but in different heights (*right*) – low-growing *V. rigida* 'Lilacina' (violet) and *V.r.* 'Polaris' (light blue) being mixed with the much taller *Verbena bonariensis*.

Various hedging plants, along with others, have been used here for parterre decoration, mostly inspired by reading books. *Left:* Rosemary Verey based her knot garden at Barnsley House, Gloucestershire, UK, on ideas in Gervase Markham's book of 1616, *The Countrie Farm*. She had already collected enough plants to create the inter-weaving threads (gold-edged and green boxwood and grey-leaved wall germander, *Teucrium × lucidrys*) to be set in gravel. It wasn't, however, until Verey saw the knot garden at Filoli in California, USA, that she realized how the threads in that garden had been clipped so precisely that they gave the impression of winding under, over, and through each other.

Below: Brian Porter's Sundial Garden at Filoli is true garden theatre, with a curving hedge of *Myrtus communis* 'Compacta' acting as the footlights. White tulips, *T.* 'Maureen', take centre stage supported by red and cerise kurume azaleas. It is the columns of yews and the pink-flowering cherries *Prunus × subhirtella* subsp. *tarentina* 'Pendula' which really set the stage, with a fat cylinder of bay (*Laurus nobilis*) to the right. *Right:* The box parterre at Bourton House in the Cotswolds, UK, came from a book called *Chinese Lattice Designs*. Monique and Richard Paice settled on the swirling swastika as being the easiest and most effective pattern to interpret in the garden context.

Even as I drove down the hill into the delightful garden of a castle in Belgium, I was sure of having arrived at the right address. The formal design signatures of Jacques Wirtz were already apparent. A long row of pleached limes (*top right*), rising high between a yew hedge on the drive side and a beech hedge by the canal, was only the beginning of what I had been led to expect of this garden.

Wirtz heads the eponymous firm of landscape architecture from where his sons Peter and Martin design within a similar philosophy. The Wirtzes' success owes much to the skilful use not only of yew, beech, and lime but also of boxwood and hornbeam – and water, moving and still.

The garden is vintage Jacques Wirtz. The living architecture, where vertical layers of hedges of varying texture bound sweeps of tree-dotted lawn and a semi-circular lily pond (*bottom right*), is set inside a huge natural bowl beside the castle.

The garden is overlooked by the town, and Wirtz has provided a natural screen of perimeter hedging. From upstairs in the house (*left*) in early summer, the vineyard sweep continues through the grid of box-edged beds, following the contours of the ground down to a thick beech hedge bordering the canal. Another Wirtz signature of the tall hornbeam gazebos (*centre*) adds punctuation to the view.

From the top of the "bowl" in the Belgian castle garden designed by Jacques Wirtz, the garden area nearest the house appears to be typically formal, with its yew hedges surrounding numerous flowerbeds. The castellated hedge shapes (*right*) and two yellow-leaved gleditsia trees form a focal point for this vista. This enclosed part of the garden, with its maze of brick paths and hedges, is the family's outdoor living area. There is a courtyard between it and the house.

Plants have long fascinated me: at six years old, I was comparing the smoothness of rose petals with the hairy leaves of anchusa. Another person similarly enthused from an early age is Dan Hinkley, the American nurseryman. As a child, he remembers watching the opening of a red oriental poppy from hour to hour in the woods in Michigan. I was with Christopher Lloyd while he, among others, was lecturing in Australia in 1988. One free day, I watched him kneel in the bush to inspect a very small wild flower. That is what happens: people with a passion for plants have a great affinity with them.

Horticulturists therefore have a wide range of interests: a few of them, for example, become plant hunters, the bringers of new plants to our gardens. James Compton must have wondered when he brought the blue *Corydalis flexuosa* back from Sichuan in China, whether it would actually become popular with the gardening public. It did.

Plants are the basis of most real gardens. This chapter shows them flourishing in towns, the bush, a vineyard, by the sea, in the mountains, and at a botanic garden, as well as unusual ones thriving in the garden that was created by the legendary Beth Chatto.

a passion
for plants

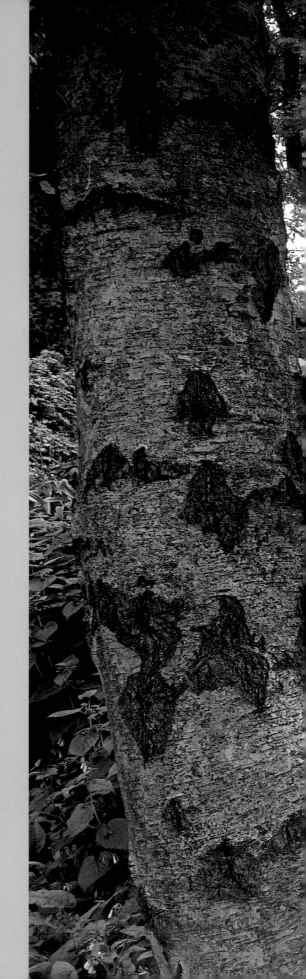

Previous pages: Beth Chatto developed her 0.6 ha (1½ acre) wood in the early 1990s. One of my favourite times there is in spring in the early morning, when sun filters through on to the rich yellow leopard's bane (*Doronicum pardalianches*).

Although Rosemary Verey was always keen to learn from contemporary garden designers, her greatest achievement was her own garden at Barnsley House, in Gloucestershire, UK, which her husband David inherited in 1951. Five years earlier, her parents-in-law had planted eight Irish yews either side of a crazy-paving path. Verey planted the full length of it with rock roses (*Helianthemum*), thus creating a spectacular effect for late spring (*above*).

Barnsley's laburnum walk (*right*) has become one of the most famous views in modern gardening. It is at the end of a 100m (100 yd) long vista that begins at the Temple and follows on from a lime walk with three rows of pleached limes on either side of a stone path. The idea came from Russell Page's 1962 book *The Education of a Gardener*. In 1964, five laburnum trees were planted either side, with purple wisteria to grow through them. In late spring, the early morning sun shines not only on the yellow laburnum flowers but also on to purple *Allium aflatunense* and yellow Welsh poppies. Stunning!

Tom Stuart-Smith is a devotee of André Le Nôtre's understanding and use of space. He is that comparative rarity: a plantsman and an innovative designer of gardens in which a visitor always feels comfortable. Stuart-Smith is well served by his fascination with garden history, and his mother's passion for plants permeated his childhood.

He designed the Broughton Grange garden, in Oxfordshire, UK, as a formal structure within the rolling landscape. From the top terrace (*top right*), surrounded by dry Mediterranean plants, the rill feeds into a square pool on the middle terrace. Around it, beech topiary provides a strange, vaguely humanoid presence. The

combination of formality and the naturalistic use of perennials and grass textures (red-flowered *Persicaria amplexicaulis* Taurus against *Calamagrostis* x *acutiflora* 'Karl Foerster') makes a luxuriant meadow (*above*) in contrast with the upper terrace.

The bottom terrace forms a large box parterre where, the pattern is based on the cellular

structure of oak, ash, and beech trees in the local landscape, magnified about 20,000 times. In spring, the parterre (*bottom right*) is filled with 5,000 tulips, among them being *T.* 'Abu Hassan', *T.* 'Prinses Irene', *T.* 'Queen of Night' (maroon black: terrific), and the occasional planting of the lily-flowered *T.* 'White Triumphator'.

Beth Chatto began her garden at Elmstead Market, in Essex, UK, in 1960 on land that had been her husband's fruit farm. As an enthusiastic amateur, Chatto had already become a collector and propagator of unusual plants and learned much from the distinguished painter and plantsman Sir Cedric Morris.

Eventually, Chatto earned her reputation while exhibiting for 12 years at the Chelsea Flower Show, London, UK, with a multi-pyramidal arrangement of plants the like of which nobody had ever seen before, winning 11 Gold medals.

Damp gardening, says Chatto, is one of the most beautiful forms, and it was to her Canal Bed (*right*) that I gravitated in the early 1980s. I watched the stream flowing past silver-leaved salixes, through candelabra primulas, yellow irises, and *Mimulus luteus*, and under large leaves of the skunk cabbage *Lysichiton americanus*. The bed was shaded by two oaks (*Quercus palustris* and *Q. robur*) with *Viburnum plicatum* f. *tomentosum* 'Mariesii' flowering on tiered branches below, and rhododendrons farther up the hill.

When the hurricane of 1987 caused widespread devastation in Badgers Wood, Chatto finally decided to make a woodland garden there (*see pp.52–3 and top left*). Her philosophy is to follow Nature (not to copy it) by putting plants together in a situation for which they are adapted. *Primula japonica* at the end of the wood, surrounded by pale pink spikes of *Persicaria bistorta* 'Superba' and the blue-green leaves of *Hosta sieboldiana elegans*, are testament to her skills.

In the gravel garden are golden-flowered *Iris* 'Benton Arundel' (*bottom left*) underneath a sumach tree and surrounded by catmint.

One Sunday in the early 1990s I found Beth Chatto alone in her garden at Elmstead Market in what used to be the car park. She was slinging yellow hosepipes into shapes that were to form the gravel garden. Chatto then began planting "exclamation marks" such as a 'Skyrocket' juniper and a Mount Etna broom and selecting plants that survive in free-draining soil with little summer rain. Two or three years later, the gravel garden had become a sensation.

In late spring you will find globular heads of *Allium hollandicum* 'Purple Sensation', with *Euphorbia characias* subsp. *wulfenii* to the left and strong tussocks of the grass *Poa labillardierei* on the right (*left*). In between the alliums and the grass are thick-stemmed *Nectaroscordum siculum*, with reddish purple bells (*right*), and aquilegias in the foreground.

In late summer, long-flowering ivory-white spikes of *Kniphofia* 'Little Maid' stand out against flat heads of *Sedum spectabile* 'Brilliant', with *Miscanthus sinensis* 'Yakujima' flowers stretching high up (*below*).

I'd been hearing about Helen Dillon's uninhibited enthusiasm for plants some time before I flew to see her garden in Dublin, Ireland. Some 20 years ago she became a "born-again gardener", advising everybody about colour control. This was as a result of a visit to the Italian Garden at Mount Stewart, Ireland, where she learned afresh after studying the beds planted in vibrant colour schemes. Dillon talks about gardening "with a bucket and back-up" – her husband being the back-up.

In her garden she has replaced the lawn with a 45cm (18in) deep canal (*top left*). The terrace is in hammered stone (slip-proof), and the canal surround is in Irish limestone with a darker polished rim. On either side of the canal, there is a long border. One is for cool colours (*centre*): *Campanula lactiflora*, monkshood (*Aconitum carmichaelii*), *Galega officinalis*, *Penstemon* 'Alice Hindley', and *Perovskia atriplicifolia*. The other border is for really hot, vibrant stuff (*above*): *Crocosmia* 'Lucifer', red roses and red dahlias, magenta-pink loosestrife (*Lythrum*), orange *Lilium henryi*, and red *Dahlia* 'Murdoch'.

Dillon doesn't have much time for conservatories: the humidity is uncomfortable, she says, and the red spider mite loves them. A greenhouse is different, however, in that it can be ventilated frequently. The Dillon version, built by her local carpenter, has the added touch of a finial that she found in a junk shop in her native Scotland (*bottom left*).

At the end of the 1980s, much of the talk at a garden conference in Melbourne, Australia, was of English gardens. Typical are these, created by two countrywomen of East Anglia. *Above:* Denny Swete was brought up in Essex, UK, and inherited her mother's commitment to gardening. She was also inspired by Penelope Hobhouse's garden at Tintinhull House, in Somerset, UK.

To my mind, when clouds of *Crambe cordifolia* appear in any garden, the summer has fully arrived. At Shore Hall, in Essex,

UK, the crambe set the standard for the rest of the garden, looking even more brilliant at dawn and by being surrounded by angelica and white valerian.

Bottom right: Lady (Xa) Tollemache at Helmingham Hall, Suffolk, UK, has a passion for plants in general. She compares garden design to painting a picture that she never finishes. It's a thrill when a new idea works well – such as putting blue love-in-a-mist (*Nigella damascena* 'Miss Jekyll') together with green-striped *Gladiolus* 'The Bride' (*top centre*). Another successful

combination is to be found in the walled garden's double border, where red oriental poppy is surrounded by *Thalictrum aquilegiifolium* 'White Cloud' and spikes of *Phormium tenax.*

The formal parterre (*top right*) at Helmingham owes a great deal not only to careful management of the boxwood topiary but also to the mass planting of only three plants: the annual white *Cosmos* 'Sonata White' and grey-leaved *Santolina chamaecyparissus* with pink *Pelargonium* 'Copthorne' flowing from the urns.

These two French country gardens created 50 years apart, in the south and the north, allow for contrasted expression.
Bottom left: Following 30 high-profile years in landscape architecture, in 2000 Pascal Cribier was commissioned by a Belgian entrepreneur with a country château in Provence, France, as well as a passion for plants, to crystallize the ideas in his garden. Already existing were lines of grapevines and fruit trees, so Cribier, who is constantly reinventing his design philosophy, built on the strips theme.

Cherry, apricot, and plum trees now follow through to the chateau. They are underplanted (*top left*) with strips of blue and white irises, interspersed with rock roses and, nearby, alternating blocks of grey-green and lime-coloured ballota.

The unevenly rounded stones of the path (*top centre*), here interplanted in the cracks with spikes of *Gladiolus byzantinus*, were designed by Cribier, who dyed the concrete stones to resemble arid conditions. Beside the path are drought-tolerant *Cistus* × *argenteus* 'Peggy Sammons' and euphorbias planted opposite silver-leaved *Elaeagnus* 'Quicksilver'.
Right: In Normandy, France, the owner of Château de Pontrancart has been designing his garden, since 1950. He enjoys naturalistic planting (with tall grasses and spots of colourful phlox around

the natural pool), as well as deep beds of single colours. In his red border (*far right*) bronze-pink *Sedum* 'Autumn Joy' (yet to flower) is surrounded by blooms of *Antirrhinum* 'Rocket', *Lobelia cardinalis*, *Phlox paniculata* 'Bright Eyes', and *Dahlia* 'Hall Park' with, below, red impatiens and mixed red verbena. This is a unique mix of perennial and annual flowers.

Some 40 miles south of Paris, France, the Chateau de Courances, whose estate dates back to the 15th century, stands surrounded by a moat in the middle of a formal park. However, it gives the impression more of a family home than a classical showplace.

Unexpected in such surroundings is the informal Japanese garden (*right*) created 75 years ago by Berthe de Behague, Marquise de Ganay, the grandmother of the Marquis de Ganay who, with his wife, the Marquise, are the garden's present owners.

At that time it was devoted entirely to rare plants. During my autumn visit I spotted two specimens of *Parrotia persica* with their golden autumn foliage and, on the right, a red maple *Acer palmatum*. Between them, in the true perspective of time, is a modern Japanese-style bridge, designed by Markus Hansen, and created by the English woodmaking-artist Giles Thomas in the early 1990s.

Like his parents, Dr Peter Valder is a global collector of rare plants. He was raised at Nooroo, in Mount Wilson, and if you want to be cool in Australia this is the place to be, more than 1,000m (3,000ft) up in the Blue Mountains of New South Wales. When we met, he was looking after Nooroo at the same time as lecturing at Sydney University. Since then, he has written three authoritative books on wisterias, Chinese gardens, and Chinese plants, all of which involved a great deal of travelling so he had to sell the family home.

The garden at Nooroo, now owned by Doctors Tony and Lorraine Barrett, is full of trees and plants, mostly arranged either side of informal paths (*left*). The only formal garden here used to be a tennis court. Valder planted 28 wisterias (*below*), which he helped to become standards by supporting their canopies on horizontal conduits painted black. Below them are pots of azaleas and small rhododendrons mixed with clematis.

One evening, as a fine drizzle started, almost covering the eucalypts on the other side of the summerhouse, I asked to be excused from the supper table. Sheltering underneath a pergola of *Wisteria sinensis* 'Jako' (*right*), and taking in the red maple, rhododendrons, and azaleas, I told myself that this was one of the world's special places.

William Martin is a plantsman who takes pleasure in planting structure and says that he is not keen on the British way of gardening: I could see that in his garden at Wigandia, in the dry bush of western Victoria, Australia – and even in his impersonation of lava with mass plantings of the silver-leaved, orange tubular-flowered *Cotyledon orbiculata* "flowing" down the hillside, past spikey *Doryanthes palmeri* (*left*).

Having lovingly nurtured his garden at Wigandia on the red volcanic scoria of Mount Noorat, Scottish-born Martin expounds his theories in characteristic terms. He has a genius for making drought-tolerant plants work together and survive on comparatively little rain, and he admits to being most inspired by his own work.

The vista from the back door at Wigandia, with its industrial hoops decorating the gate (*bottom centre*), has a big *Yucca elephantipes* setting the scene in front of the landscape, while by the front gate the corrugated iron, which Martin describes as "white fella's bark", is a reminder of its role in Australia's structural history. Here, though, it is decorated with agaves and grasses (*Poa labillardierei*) on the ground and Irish spurge in a container on top (*top centre*).

Elsewhere, Martin had once piled large cuttings of cactus on wooden saw-horses and forgot about them until they started to grow legs, unconnected to the ground (*far right*). So, he moved them in among his sedums (*S.* 'Autumn Joy') and "bushes" of *Salvia canariensis*, and left them there. Wigandia's skilful eccentricity is a triumph.

When Molly Chappellet first saw her new vineyard home high up over the Napa valley in California, USA, nearly 40 years ago, any misgivings she might have had about the practicalities – both natural and domestic – of living there were swept away by the view. "The surrounding hills, the lake below, the wooded acreage all around", she wrote in her book *A Vineyard Garden*, "are still my favourite parts of the property."

The ranch-style house, at that time, was airless and hot, and so the need for shade and vegetables inspired the first steps in making the garden. Here, surrounded by hills, with Lake Hennessy beyond, Chappellet's enthusiasm for going one step farther and still farther, with more and more plants, produced the present garden design.

The herb garden (*top left*) includes rue (*Ruta graveolens,* the herb of grace) in yellow flower, chives (*Allium schoenoprasum*), thyme (*Thymus vulgaris*), and woodruff in the foreground, and is edged with grey-leaved lambs' ears (*Stachys byzantina*). To the left, hand-split stakes from the vineyard are used to make trellises for all kinds of beans.

On a late spring morning near the Chenin Blanc vineyard, clusters of yellow-green blooms of *Euphorbia characias* subsp. *wulfonii* and clusters of *Erysimum* 'Bowles' Mauve' appear through the mist (*bottom left*). Nearby, unidentified bearded irises, given by a friend, grow through catmint (*bottom centre*).

Farther down the garden, two *Ailanthus altissima* (Tree of heaven), budding out in the setting of a rocky outcrop, rise among densely planted artichokes and cardoons. French lavender (*Lavandula stoechas*) and feathery bronze fennel show off among them (*right*).

Dan Hinkley's phenomenal success as a nurseryman, with his partner the former architect Robert Jones at Heronswood, in Washington State, USA, has as much to do with his flair for good judgement and being excellent company as with his plant-hunting expeditions abroad.

On arrival at Heronswood, which is set among Douglas firs on the Kitsap peninsula, I plunged into the woodland garden among the hunter's treasures. Filling the space around earthen paths is a massive collection of trees and shrubs (magnolias, maples, camellias, and hydrangeas, including the real show-off *Hydrangea paniculata* 'Heronswood Giant'). Half way through the woodland garden, a ruined grotto (*below*) appears among the trees. It was created by Little & Lewis.

Still searching, I found the ultimate in "spectacular" plants – a long-stemmed perennial with masses of green umbrella-like leaves, mottled variously in black, burgundy, pink, and green. This turned out to be *Peltiphyllum delavayi*, which Hinkley brought back from Thundering Cave Terrace at 2,740m (9,000ft) in Sichuan, China, in 1996.

Near the house (*right*), a weeping Japanese larch (*Larix kaempferi*) rises above the New Zealand sedge *Carex comans*. To the left of the path, the fragrant white flowers of *Ozothamnus rosmarinifolius* confirmed the soft green look. The colour of late summer perennials appears further round the path in this exhilarating place.

Carol Skinner was first inspired by reading Gertrude Jekyll and Margery Fish more than 30 years ago. It was Jekyll's concept of the cottage style of gardening that encouraged her and her husband Malcolm to find their idyllic 17th-century cottage deep in the fertile Worcestershire countryside in England.

I first went to Eastgrove Cottage Garden in 1990, when the garden was already well established with mature trees and hedges, two greenhouses, brick paths, and the rock bank wall ("The Great Wall of China") – all built by her husband. They had created together the different areas around the cottage while Skinner was still experimenting with some of the planting. She was in a natural-istic period, when beds of pink-flecked *Salvia sclarea*, the fuzzy grey foliage of the wormwood *Artemisia absinthium* 'Lambrook Silver', and rose campion (*Lychnis coronaria*) were planted on the other side of the hedge from a selection of red and pink penstemons (*top right*).

The rock bank (*bottom right*) sports many of Skinner's favourite species, including *Olearia* × *scilloniensis* below the apple tree, and *Lotus hirsutus* with, as the name suggests, hairy grey leaves and pink-flushed, creamy white flowers, below the cottage window.

One of Skinner's special areas looks at its best each late spring, when the yellow cups of *Paeonia mlokosewitschii* are surrounded by *Euphorbia palustris*, grey-blue cardoon spikes, *Tulipa* 'Queen of Night', and *T.* 'Magier' (*left*). The pale peony colour carries on to the yellow thuja bush on the left, and in the evening light to *Cornus alternifolia* 'Argentea'. The flowering cherry on the right is *Prunus* 'Shôgetsu'.

I cannot believe that there is another garden in the world where a supreme genius for creative planting has a more sympathetic, exquisitely designed house around which to create a planting than Christopher Lloyd's garden at Great Dixter in East Sussex, UK. The house was restored nearly a century ago by Sir Edwin Lutyens for Nathaniel Lloyd, father of Christopher, the internationally admired and emulated gardener. Nathaniel Lloyd was keen on topiary and designed a "Parliament" of ten

yew peacocks (*bottom right*). Set against Lutyens' chimneys, they are the setting for fluffy hedges of *Aster lateriflorus* 'Horizontalis', the other side of which are different heights of *Cortaderia selloana*, *Canna* 'Wyoming', and *Miscanthus sinensis*.

The meadow below the house, full of daffodils in mid-spring, also includes the delightful snakes head fritillaries (*Fritillaria meleagris*) and the white version *F.m. alba* along with white *Anemone nemorosa* (*top centre*).

Christopher Lloyd has always pushed the boundaries of

horticulture, constantly seeking new plants. Since Fergus Garrett joined him as head gardener about 12 years ago, they have bounced ideas around between them on how to plant the garden at Great Dixter.

As if producing another ace, Lloyd decided to replace his old rose garden with the Exotic Garden (*above*). Here, dahlias (unfashionable hitherto) such as red *D.* 'Witteman's Superba' and yellow *D.* 'Davar Donna' rise through heart-shaped leaves of *Polymnia sonchifolia*. Leaves of Japanese banana (*Musa basjoo*)

arch over the top of *Verbena bonariensis*, while red palmate leaves of *Ricinus communis* 'Carmencita' rise on the left.

The floral scene around the front door of Great Dixter (*top right*) is the epitome of welcome. After a walk down the path with the meadow either side, pots of rudbeckias, begonias, pelargoniums, and salvias make an unforgettable sight.

Here are three atmospheric gardens, one of them lovingly inherited while the other two were created by the owners. *Above:* Sue Nathan's ideas for planting the lakeside bank at Bonython Manor in Cornwall, UK, were derived from the prairie garden at Lady Farm (*see pp.156–7*). She planted red-spiked *Crocosmia masoniorum* through red drifts of *Stipa arundinacea*, while on the far side of the lake orange cannas, yellow rudbeckias, and yuccas appear through waves of billowing red grass.
Right: Although Anne Chambers was brought up at Kiftsgate Court in Gloucestershire, UK,

she has made it her own garden, reflecting skills as a plantswoman (and, in the lower garden as a designer). She has planted *Lilium regale* and red *Rosa* 'Europeana' so that they are perfectly offset by the portico to the house.
Far right: Arnaud Maurières and Eric Ossart were influenced by Roberto Burle Marx and Luis Barragán in their design of Jardin des Paradis at Cordes-sur-Ciel, France. Here they have achieved a garden that satisfies all of the senses. In the quiet of a misty morning by the lower pool, pots of *Agapanthus* 'Blue Giant' are lined up parallel to shorter *Tulbaghia violacea*, mimicking them on the other side.

These American plantsmen and women live on the east coast of the USA. *Below:* Nick and Penny Harris's garden is at Smallidge Point on the rocky Maine coast, facing across the Atlantic. There, they have created a cutting garden from what had been half of a tennis court. With red and white Shirley poppies, foxgloves, dahlias, lavender, and sunflowers growing happily in raised beds, Penny Harris has made a delightful garden. It is surrounded by a fence of original design, which at the same time is eminently practical. Painted turquoise-grey, the fence effectively filters the wind and keeps out the local deer, while acting as a neutral background to the flowers.

Top right: Lynden Miller has spent the last 20 or more years transforming city parks and gardens in New York City. She was originally an artist, but then took courses at the New York Botanical Garden before moving to England and meeting famous gardeners and designers. "When I went to England", she told me, "I was a painter who gardened. When I returned to New York, I became a gardener who painted with plants."

Miller is committed to decorating public spaces in New York with mass planting of different shapes, colours, and textures. The repaving of the Perennial Garden at the New York Botanical Garden has afforded wider borders and new beds, allowing Miller even more scope near the Enid A. Haupt Conservatory to demonstrate her original plant combinations. *Gomphrena* 'Strawberry Fields' has bright red, strawberry-like flower heads growing behind *Iris laevigata* 'Variegata', set against the mauve flowers of *Aster novae-angliae* (*bottom centre*). Here, Miller also encouraged bright red *Hibiscus* 'Lord Baltimore' to grow through the dark bronze-red foliage of castor oil plant *Ricinus communis* 'Carmencita' (*bottom right*).

Two women gardeners in Essex, UK, both of them aficionados of Beth Chatto since the 1970s, share a compulsive love of plants several kilometres apart, aided and abetted by sympathetic husbands. *Left:* When, at the age of 21, Sue Staines made her first garden, she realized that gardening was and is an instinctive art form and not a craft. Years later Staines and her husband developed 1.4ha (3½ acres) of lawns around plant-filled island beds at Glen Chantry.

Alpines feature strongly in the rock garden, which is surrounded effectively by a woodland of specimen trees – *Cornus controversa* 'Aurea' in flower among them. *Asplenium scolopendrium, Sisyrinchium idahoense*, and *Chrysanthemum weyrichii* edge the pool, which is surrounded by golden grass *Carex elata* 'Aurea', pink *Astrantia major* 'Roma', shuttlecock fern (*Matteuccia struthiopteris*), and *Rodgersia pinnata*.

In early autumn, trees emphasize the planting structure, with *Prunus sargentii* turning orange-red over the dry brook and the foliage of paper-bark maple (*Acer griseum*) changing into orange, red, and then scarlet, by the bridge (*bottom right*). *Top right:* Jill Cowley's tastes have diversified since she first encountered the Beth Chatto revolution. Chatto is not a great rose fan but Cowley is. Indeed, roses are the signature theme at Park Farm, where a specimen rose in one area might appear as ground cover in another. *Rosa* 'Blairii No. 2' cascades down into blue-purple spires of *Polemonium pulcherrimum* on one side of a brick path, opposite palest pink 'Stanwell Perpetual' roses. Columns of junipers lead on towards her husband's pavilion, decorated with traditional, white bargeboards.

In his *International Book of Trees*, Hugh Johnson, paraphrasing Charles Darwin, writes that "A traveller should be a botanist, for in most views trees form the chief embellishment." He goes on to say that, of all plants, they are the ones that dictate the atmosphere in a garden.

When Johnson and his wife Judy bought Saling Hall, in Essex, UK, in 1970, it was backed by "immemorial" elm trees, 15 of them being 27–30m (90–100ft) high. Four years later, all of them were obliterated by Dutch elm disease, which destroyed so much of the English landscape. The loss of the elms decided the character of two-thirds of the 4.8ha (12 acres) at Saling Hall, even though its walled garden, with apple trees, roses, and perennials, was the pivotal part of the garden.

Johnson then began an arboretum by planting willows, pines, and oaks on chalky boulder clay. "I was mad", he says, but here, years later, were *Sorbus sargentiana* in autumn foliage with, on the left, *Prunus avium* 'Plena' and, on the right, the yellow leaves of *Toona sinensis* and the red swamp cypress (*Taxodium distichum*) (*top left*). "Trees *like* other trees", remarks Johnson, "they shelter each other."

In mid-summer, a water jet completes the sylvan atmosphere of a secluded water garden among Caucasian maples (*bottom left*).

Johnson also dug the "Red Sea" – a pond with a birch-planted peninsula jutting into it. There, *Acer rubrum* looks spectacular in early October sun and frost (*right*).

David Hicks made his first complete garden in Suffolk, aged 26, and soon became known as an international interior and garden designer, with a love of straight lines and symmetry.

In his own garden at The Grove, in Oxfordshire, UK, he had no time for herbaceous borders, yet at Stellenberg, near Cape Town, South Africa, he devised a walled garden of roses and perennials within clipped parterres, complementing the beautiful Cape Dutch house.

Sandy Ovenstone, who was given the garden as a silver wedding present by her husband Andrew, is a natural gardener, and the scheme which Hicks and she worked on together was very simple. It was divided in two by a brick path and a rose tunnel of *Rosa* 'The New Dawn' (*right*) running between a new grotto and a wall fountain, with symmetrical but dissimilar square beds on each side. These became grids of myrtle, clipped every three weeks. They were then filled with perennials such as delphiniums, foxgloves, irises, teucrium, and dianthus (*below*) with David Austin roses such as the red *Rosa* L.D. Braithwaite and the light pink *R*. Heritage.

Sheila Boardman's passion for the scents of France – lavender and roses – is undiminished, as can be seen in her garden at Northwind, in Cape Town's Constantia, South Africa. More than 20 years ago, Boardman began her new garden by removing 40 trees as well as two rows of vines. In the vines' place, on one side of the garden, she planted a 64m (70yd) long lavender walk, using *Lavandula angustifolia* to brilliant effect (*right*). She tapered it to create an illusion of even greater vista length, stretching towards the landscape and the mountains beyond – another French effect on which Boardman is keen.

Inspired by Lady Salisbury's East Garden at Hatfield House, in Hertfordshire, UK, which she describes as "strong and clever", Boardman made a garden of long paths and mixed beds surrounded by low hedges of myrtle. These became the main structure and perspective of a vista running parallel to the vine walk.

From the house, the view runs past an armillary sphere to the focal point of the garden – the circular pond. In it stands a bronze sculpture of a wattled crane enhanced by at least seven Alhambra-like water jets (*below*). Old-fashioned roses, on which Boardman is "mad keen", surround the pool. She also trained myrtle into topiary shapes using delicate wire frames that she had originally found in France.

The art of Minimalism, which promoted simplicity in painting and architecture, emerged in the 1950s. Some of the landscape architect Thomas Church's garden designs had already demonstrated an ultra-simplicity, as with the sensuous curves of the El Novillero garden in California. Andrea Cochran's ASLA award-winning roof garden in San Francisco similarly rejoices in undulating curves of metal waves.

Minimalism soon influenced the world of garden design via the exterior work of the great Mexican architect Luis Barragán. Steve Martino now adapts Barragán's style to include the use of desert plants. Nothing could be more sensuous or tactile than such a combination of shapes and textures.

The flowing curves of many kinds of materials, along with the lines of geometric patterns and simple planting, allow for a wide varieties of ideas. There are Christopher Bradley-Hole's intricate structures, lushly planted, as well as the designs of Vladimir Sitta, who produces ever more astonishing schemes and devices. Topher Delaney's creations are full of artistic enthusiasm, while the stonework of Shunmyo Masuno reflects his erudite mind.

sensuous minimalism

Previous pages: On the terrace of a penthouse in San Francisco, USA, Andrea Cochran has designed a roof-top impression of the hills of northern California. Low containers, crammed with sedums, stand out against a yellow wall and the grass *Stipa tenuissima*.

Until the 1930s, most landscape architects in the USA were seen as glorified gardeners but Thomas Church established a new status. According to the landscape architect Richard McPherson, "All the gardens we now create in California are based on the concepts and philosophies of Thomas Church: we just don't know it".
Church never imposed a design on the owners but created an environment that moved from the inside of the house to the outside, in sympathy with its architecture and the surrounding topography.
Right: In this Minimalist garden with the three-lobed pool Church positioned the pool so it was the main feature in the garden yet effectively softened its shape, as did the curving rose pergola. Church designed this garden for a 1930s' property in Berkeley, California, USA, in the late 1940s.

Bottom: In the 1950s, Church designed a garden for a modern house near San Francisco, USA. It contained sweeps of unpolished terrazzo paving surrounding the blue-green pool and trees beyond. The nearby figurine, said Church, should be large enough to be seen but not so large that it overshadows the planting: was this sowing the seed of garden minimalism?

The Moorish architecture of North Africa and southern Spain formed the original influence in the work of minimalist Luis Barragán. In the 1970s, his disciple Steve Martino, working in the middle of the Sonoran desert, expanded on Barragán's style of garden design when he realized that the hitherto unrecognized beauty of desert plants had colour, texture, and form. From them he could create sustainable gardens, which fit into the desert landscape.

Left: Barragán's mastery of space, light, and shadow is shown in the design of his roof "garden" at Casa Barragán, his late 1940s' home in Mexico City. Mexico. It is composed solely of vertical and horizontal lines, with stark walls painted in terracotta, purple, and white.

Right: One of Martino's first gardens was for Cliff Douglas' Arid Zone Trees nursery in Arizona, USA. There, in homage to Barragán, Martino designed an orange, sidewinder-like serpentine wall, leading to Douglas' office. Thriving plants here are the octopus agave *A. vilmoriniana*, red-flowered *Penstemon parryi*, and the desert marigold *Baileya multiradiata*.

Below: Elsewhere in Phoenix, Arizona, USA, Barragán set up this view of Camelback Mountain, which appears over a cobalt-blue wall decorated by rusted, steel fountain panels. The view, which is overhung by yellow-flowered palo verde trees (*Parkinsonia florida*), is from the home of people who were enthused by minimalism after having visited Casa Barragán.

"My walls are always functional", says Steve Martino and so they are: a blue one to shore up a hillside in Tucson (*see p.4*), a raised rill to do the same (see p.23), another as a serpentine terracotta screen (*see p.99*), and, in Las Vegas, a curvy red fireplace on the terrace of a private house. "But they don't have to be vertical", says this minimalist designer, "I'm bored with that." Martino is creating sculpture, whether he knows it or not, that is shapely, angular, sometimes shocking – and colourful.

Left: The terrace in Las Vegas, Nevada, USA, overlooks a golf course, which is partly screened by palo verde trees. The occasional container has been introduced, with the owners finding red pelargoniums to match the wall colour. Martino might, instead, have chosen a shrub such as Mexican flame bush (*Calliandra tweedii*), which has red stamens arranged in axillary, spherical heads (*below*).

Top right: Strong colours and contrast are all part of the Luis Barragán theme with which Martino has become identified as a minimalist. In the Arid Zone Trees (AZT) nursery garden in Arizona, USA, Martino was again influenced by Barragán, whose vividly textured surfaces, whether plaster, timber, or water, were all part of his principle of working with the elements.

It would be interesting to see Barragán's reaction to Martino's green mosaic-tiled wall, which winds across the courtyard behind the AZT offices. In the desert, this shiny river of tiles suggests cooling water in the heat of the desert sun. I hope Barragán would also have liked Martino's shark fins sculpture (*bottom right*), painted purple, on the far side. He would, I am sure, have enjoyed the rows of square orange columns either side of the gate, interspersed with agave-coloured wooden posts as well as agaves themselves.

The three gardens either side of the central garden were directly influenced by the work of Luis Barragán, whose work the central garden is.

Left: Ricardo Legoretta designed a city home with a series of outdoor courtyards in Mexico City, Mexico. The most subtle of all is the entry yard, where a wall fountain trickles on to the stone floor of a shallow pool designed by the painter Vicente Rojo. He used concentric circles, of two tones of volcanic stone, grey and burnt ochre, thus increasing the sense of visual movement.

Centre: The Chapel for the Capuchinas Sacramentarias in Tlalpan, Mexico City, was designed by Luis Barragán as a present for the nuns in the early 1950s and is one of his best-known works. The inner garden, surrounded by high walls, is a symbol of silence, while sunlight falls on the black stone fountain, the yellow lattice, and at midday the black rock floor.

Top right: John Douglas, who worked with Steve Martino on the Arid Zones Trees nursery project (*see pp.99 and 101*), created a raised water rill for the Kitchell family in Phoenix, Arizona, USA. It is set amid desert plants such as prickly pear (*Opuntia ficus-indica*) and fairy duster (*Calliandra californica*).

Bottom right: Steve Martino's raised pool in the entry courtyard of this spatial garden, in Phoenix, Arizona, produces attractive shadows at dusk. The sculptural plants and the sounds of the fountain, all shaded by a custom-designed awning, add to the overall effect.

Steve Martino and Ted Smyth have both interpreted the surroundings to these gardens in a typical Minimalist style. *Below:* Anyone hiring Martino is probably living somewhere in the Sonoran desert, where a swimming pool is *de rigeur*. In the Tucson foothills, in Arizona, USA, where this garden overlooks the city and the hills beyond, Harris' hawks glide lazily around and lesser night hawks fly circuits and dip in the pools. Martino, naturally, designed the ultimate Minimalist arbour to resemble a hawk in flight at the side of the infinity pool.

Instead of strong Barragán colour, Martino adopted that of the desert stone with which he built the raised reflecting pool, filled by the fish fountain (*left*). Reflected in it are the yellow flowers of the native, Arizona brittlebush (*Encelia farinosa*).

Right: Barragán-admirer Ted Smyth, who works in Auckland, New Zealand, began as a graphic artist and painter. By the 1980s, however, he had become passionate about landscape design, observing Barragán's use of space and light. His geometric design is a development of that.

Within the pool framework of stone terraces, the linear fountains are part of Smyth's design vocabulary, a controlled expression of water in movement. "I am not interested in frothy, splashy things", he says. The arches, with lintels underlit in reference to Smyth's earlier rainbow paintings, contain the garden spatially while drawing in the country beyond. The stillness is enhanced by the soft greens and greys of *Dracaena draco*, cycads, and *Lavandula canariensis*.

As soon as garden designer Cilla Cooper moved into her new home, on the north shore of Auckland, New Zealand, she knew that the picket fence and the wooden bridge in the front of the house would have to make way for something else. The result is pure Minimalist theatre à la Luis Barragán.

Cooper's watery front garden is now surrounded by a series of purple-grey walls with spaces in between, through which a few subtropical plants and trees appear (*top left*). These are sufficient to naturalize the garden.

The main design feature is a broad bridge of industrial aluminium, constructed diagonally across the water, with a white nude sculpture in the pool on one side (*bottom left*) and a waterfall on the other (*right*). At dusk, fibre optics dramatize the whole scene with lighting in the pool (*below*) and on the waterfall, gradually rotating at intervals through blue, red, green, white, and yellow hues.

Minimalism is typified both by Piet Boon's house and his garden near Amsterdam. Piet is one of the Netherlands' most talked-about modern designers, and although he is primarily known as an architect his creativity has disseminated into other areas. It was hardly surprising then that when he and his stylist wife Karin came to design a new house for their young family they wanted to "shock a little". As the house is constructed of various materials, including a zinc roof, it was natural that the garden should follow suit.

Piet designed a long, charcoal-grey, raised pool surrounded by a wooden deck between the courtyard and the pool house (*top left*). Such simplicity required a planting design that fitted happily with the surrounding fields.

Garden designer Piet Oudolf, a friend of the Boons, chose to make a graphic design in which the structure of the garden and its planting form a strong supporting role to the house. He had the idea of flanking the pool with vast block plantings of the soft golden grass *Deschampsia cespitosa* 'Goldtau' (*below*). He then inset them with a block each side of tightly planted junipers – each block cut shorter than the height of the grasses (*bottom left*).

On one side of the garden, he mass-planted an Oudolf-signature row of perennials and, on the other side, cloud hedges of beech and boxwood. The pool-side of the courtyard has portals of standard wisterias growing in four boxwood-planted cubes (*bottom centre*).

Meeting landscape architect Shunmyo Masuno, head priest of Yokohama's Kenko-ji Temple in Japan, showed me yet another dimension to the art of Minimalist gardening.

"It is because I was born into a Zen family", he told me "that I became a landscape architect." Stones, Masuno believes, have a spiritual life as much as plants and animals, and in a Zen garden they become the most important element. This is the language of *karesansui*, the dry-stone garden, and the gardens Masuno creates retain a deep spirituality.

This is evident at the Canadian Embassy, sited opposite a wooded park in Aoyama, Tokyo, Japan, where in 1990 Masuno was entrusted to create a garden. Hewn rocks are one of Masuno's innovations in Zen garden design, and his love of stone gave him the idea of portraying the broad landscape of Canada, coast to coast (*far left*). At its simplest, long splits of rock, with rows of wedge holes left as they were, represent the ancient Canadian Shield, while the Rocky Mountains in the west are represented by the pyramid sculpture.

One of Masuno's most significant landscapes was completed for the Cerulean Tower Tokyu Hotel, Tokyo, Japan, in 2001. The concept of the garden, called Kanza-tei, "sitting in tranquillity", is of waves rolling against the hotel "shore" (*bottom centre*). Terraces of white granite, many edged with wedging grooves, represent the waves (*top centre*). Farther along, while seated at breakfast, I enjoyed observing the intricately designed slopes (*right*) made of differing textures, tones, and shapes of granite. These are darker than the stone of the "waves". All in all, Masuno's idea is inspirational.

Depending on which era they come from, some people describe Vladimir Djurovic's work as "using the borrowed landscape", while others describe it as "topographical larceny". Either way, what the Beirut landscape architect with a Slovak name enjoys best is to create environments that bring people closer to nature but within the Minimalist tradition.

The clients for Djurovic's ordered designs are likely to be young, aware, and well-off, with a sense of wanting to enjoy the outdoor as well as the indoor life. Like Elie Saab, Lebanon's leading *haute couture* designer, who owns this mountain retreat in Faqra, Lebanon, Djurovic's clients want to have space, to breathe and to rejuvenate.

Tailor-made for contemplation, the garden has been created so that earth, water, and fire can be brought together in this landscape. Recessed sitting areas built from local stone and interspersed with long, thin lines of grass, align the eye level with the raised pool surface. On cool evenings a hidden button ignites the two fires on either side (*right*). Is this a sensuous idea? In the rain, it most certainly is.

As well as Minimalist, Vladimir Djurovic's work is often described as Zen. If this is seen as enlightenment through meditation and insight, then his gardens have the right ambience for it. For Djurovic, a filmman's commission to create a quiet space that wraps around a modern apartment several floors up outside Beirut, in Lebanon, was a real challenge. The task was particularly difficult as the entire garden is only 4m (12ft) wide around the apartment, and it is surrounded on three sides by unsightly buildings, which required screening.

The view from the stone seating area, which benefits visually from dramatic shadows, is straight along the main axis (*right*). A scented gardenia hedge lines the outer side of five long stone strips, with grass between (evidently a Djurovic trademark) before you reach a long lawn open to the wide view over Beirut, protected by glass balustrades. Two decorative tangerine trees frame the view of the city from inside the house.

The illusory effect of water, says Djurovic, plays a vital role in enlarging space, as seen from the garden and the house. The Jacuzzi (*top left*) takes on this role of visual expansion while merging through subtle channels with the lap pool (*bottom left*) around the corner. The lush planting of palm trees (*Archontophoenix alexandrae*) and the lance-shaped leaves of *Strelitzia reginae* set among *Carissa grandiflora* effectively provides a lush garden for two aspects of the house.

The Minimalist landscape
architect Bet Figueras worked
alongside architect Oscar
Tusquets when, in 1997, they
redesigned the garden of this
15th-century villa set high
on a hill overlooking the
Mediterranean, near
Barcelona, in Spain.

They brought contemporary
design to several parts of the
28ha (70 acre) hillside, including
the creation of a labyrinth,
sweeping stone steps, and
walkways. In doing this, they
were influenced by a mixture of
Arab and classical designs by,
for example, Leon Battista
Alberti, an architect of the Italian
Renaissance who thought that a
house that enjoyed a wide view
should also have a garden that
becomes not only an extension
of the house but also a link with
the landscape beyond.

It was at the front of the
house, however, that I found the
most spectacular Minimalist
designs in Figueras' and
Tusquets' use of water, stonework,
and the simple planting. A single
fountain (*right*) jets out of
a shallow pool at the top of
a garden slope. It is enclosed
above by a semi-circle of English
oaks (*bottom left*) and, below, a
water garden stretches between
it and the house. From the
fountain, parallel channels of
water (*top left*) flow between
terraces of reconstituted
crushed stone, planted with
dichondra in strips, to the main
house via a long, wide rill with
shallow waterfalls every 4m
(4yd). The ochre-painted
colonnade surely has its origins
in the design of ancient forums.

The water in the four
ornamental pools (*top centre*)
outside recirculates on
successive levels through
a series of underground
tunnels, as in Roman times.

Kristof Swinnen's spare, Minimalist style is very much in evidence in Ingrid Coene's garden for her modernist house, which backs on to open country and a cattle field near Antwerp, Belgium. Swinnen learned how to make garden architecture with plants by studying for four years with the landscape architect Jacques Wirtz in the mid-1990s.

On finding a row of willows (*Salix alba*) bordering the garden, Swinnen immediately suggested a double row. He also persuaded Coene that a pool (two pools, even) at right angles to the house would reflect the landscape. Having decided on a cruciform design, delineated by low walls of French limestone (*left*), Swinnen proposed a sunken garden so that the pools became lower with edges surrounded by lawn. This, along with the small dining area, has the visual effect of enlarging the garden.

To the left of the house, Swinnen planted a double row of pleached hornbeams. Beneath them, and one-third of the way along, are two red containers of the red grass *Imperata cylindrica* 'Rubra' (the only point of strong colour in the garden) and two cream-coloured containers of *Pennisetum orientale* (*above*).

Christopher Bradley-Hole set up his landscape practice in 1996, making a special study of perennials in urban Europe, and by 1997 he had won his first Best-in-Show at the Chelsea Flower Show, London, UK. That was for a garden of allegory and narrative, specifically designed to suggest mood.

Mood and a strong sense of space are what his Minimalist design for Gail Thorson and Tim Macklem's roof garden in north London, UK, has in plenty. Against a still-black sky, the rain glistened in bright sunshine among waving grasses, irises, and one olive tree (right). They were all in formally arranged, galvanized steel planters of differing sizes placed on gravel around a central deck of red cedar, the place for breakfast at the table (left). The roof, sited on the tallest building in

the area, provides relaxation on a floor that varies between geometrically-placed decking and gravel. The owners, who are keen gardeners, love being up here in this exceptional place.

Bradley-Hole has heightened the mood by painting different walls yellow, red, and grey (above), with tall grasses such as Calamagrostis × acutiflora 'Karl Foerster' and Miscanthus sinensis waving nearby, and, lower, Stipa tenuissima flowing over the metal containers.

Quite different from all of the other plants is a line of dwarf Japanese pines (Pinus parviflora), which flourish by the south wall.

At different stages, both Vladimir Sitta and the owners of the garden near Sydney harbour, Australia, were, Sitta says, "a little bit scared". His own approach to Minimalism, inspired by most of the arts, is theatrical. Someone left a piece of red stone in his office and, after some "doodling", Sitta asked his contractor, Michael Bates, to drive to a remote bush quarry near Alice Springs, in the Northern Territory. In the heat of mid-summer, Bates cut as much of the red sandstone as needed, more or less by himself.

Once on site back in Sydney, the sandstone had to be sawn to maintain horizontal joints. This was one of the scary bits, but it actually led to great precision. "Design should celebrate the unpredictable", says Sitta. This he has certainly achieved in the garden near Sydney harbour, which is pure, concentrated design using varying textures of stone, water … and plants such as glaucous grasses (*Festuca glauca*) and succulents (*left*).

Two other garden designs by Sitta, which are different again in style and experimentation, are on pp.136–7 and 248–9.

In California, USA, where garden design is more adventurous than in many parts of the globe, Topher Delaney is the West Coast's leading conceptualist garden designer. Conceptual art grew out of Minimalism in the 1960s, and here in a garden in Palo Alto Delaney has brought together ideas from other parts of the world to complement the house, which had recently been restyled in glass and steel.

A front garden walk between large chunks of aquamarine glass nestling in a lawn of mind-your-own-business (*Soleirolia soleirolii*) – an oblique reference to the Ryo-anji rocks in Kyoto – brings us to a glossy show of arum lilies. These are near a green glass fountain playing between hedges of lavender, as in a Mediterranean garden.

The main courtyard, of decomposed granite, boasts formally placed terracotta pots of citrus trees (a classical reference to the Medicis) beyond the dining area (*below*). Here are two thick concrete panels, one painted yellow, the other green, in Luis Barragán style. Originally they were designed for the previous house.

The terrace of polished black granite (*right*), a continuation of the interior floors, has a single olive tree set into it, while a low wall provides as a division between an even wider and longer bed of lavender and a mauve swathe of wallflowers *Erysimum* 'Bowles' Mauve' (*left*) – just another taste of the Delaney style.

A garden can inspire both fantasy and romantic feelings in many of us – fantasy being a rare illusion created by the imagination, whereas romance lifts the spirit and brings adventure and excitement to our lives. All kinds of artists and writers worldwide have celebrated gardening in their works by conjuring exuberant or romantic scenes, for example, in Titian's *Bacchanal* or in Jane Austen's novel *Pride & Prejudice*. When he created his Innisfree garden in New York State, USA, Walter Beck, a painter who loved the Orient, was inspired by 8th-century Chinese painter Wang Wei.

Some of the most persistent memories can be captured in a garden. These may be triggered by a sense of awe and excitement, such as when waking early in the morning in the sub-tropics to revel in the sights and scents of a garden that you could only have guessed at the evening before – for example, in the garden at Nindooinbah in Queensland, Australia, the unfamiliar calls of kookaburras and magpies added to the fairytale atmosphere.

fantasy
& romance

Previous pages: Walter Beck carefully positioned fantastic rock sculptures around the lotus-filled lake, at The Point, in his Innisfree garden in upstate New York, USA. The biggest one was the Owl rock – surely the most beautiful monolith at Innisfree.

I slept with the windows open until dawn and, almost immediately, emerged into the garden of Nindooinbah House, Queensland, Australia, itself both fantastic and romantic in the mist (*below*). Here, beyond a blooming jacaranda tree, was a scarlet-painted teahouse, which appeared to float on the Japanese iris-fringed lake (*right*). The teahouse was designed by the owner and landscape painter Patrick Hockey and was influenced by the style of willow-pattern china.

Nindooinbah House, which became one of the beauties of early 20th-century Queensland architecture, was originally built in the 1850s, ten years after white settlement. When driving into this sheep-station homestead in the dark of a September evening in 1987, I noticed oriental features in the gatehouse, pergolas, and cedar verandahs. These had been inspired by the first owners' Japanese honeymoon. Such exotic touches were also in evidence indoors in the extraordinary, high-ceilinged room in which I was to sleep. Hockey had recently furnished and decorated it in the most delightful, detailed style.

Garstons is an island garden devised in rolling countryside by Jenny Jones, an accomplished Australian theatre designer, with her husband Timothy O'Brien. They bought their farmhouse in the mid 1990s and immediately set about restoration, using the vast accumulated knowledge from their creative lives.

The garden is full of experimental ideas, including how it is sheltered on all sides. A mixed hedge is the first line of defence against the wind and the local four-footed creatures, but Jones also erected screens and built walls.

The most unusual feature of all, and the most romantic, is the pond house (*above*), which is the focal point of the garden at Garstons, on the Isle of Wight, UK. It is built of glass and bounded on three sides at waist level by water. Grey screens shade the roof, while oriental red blinds screen the sides. Dinner in this candle-lit setting is fantastic, and especially the scene at water level.

Three glass screens in the gravel garden (*centre*) form a "prism" which not only protects the black-stemmed bamboo *Phyllostachys nigra* but also provides reflective surfaces which make the most of the available light and colour.

There is one distinct vista, a central path running from the back gate towards the house on wooden decking and interrupted by steps two-thirds of the way down (*top right*): it has a central shining steel strip, reminiscent of a water rill. At the bottom, water trickles down stainless-steel plumb lines into a pool (*bottom right*).

Cubist fantasy was the theme chosen by Roberto Burle Marx for a garden in a valley near Petrópolis in Brazil. The house had been designed in 1954 by Oscar Niemeyer, the creator of Brasilia (capital city of Brazil), on which Burle Marx also worked. Burle Marx was not only one of the most important land-scape architects of the 20th century but also a prolific and brilliant painter and designer until he died in 1993. He became a legend as much for his generosity of spirit as for his talent for art and music.

His garden near Petrópolis fell into neglect until 2000, when it was restored to its former glory by the current owner, Gilberto Strunk. The chequerboard pattern of the lawn is in two shades of St Augustine grass – *Stenotaphrum secundatum* (dark grass) and *S.s.* 'Variegatum' (white grass) – with *Iresine herbstii* making the purple contrast (*left*). The lawn is at its most shocking when first seen from the driveway, through tall palms *Syagrus romanzoffiana* and the bromeliad *Alcantarea reginae* (*right*).

A folly pretending to be a Majapahit temple is typical of Made Wijaya's fantastic garden designs. Originally from Australia, Wijaya has lived in the Far East for more than 30 years and has been designing tropical gardens for most of that time. For Victor Ngo's private garden in Singapore, Wijaya was inspired by gardens during the golden era of Balinese Hindu temple building.

He designed a formal Bali-style pool with red-tiled pavilions (*bottom left*), in collaboration with architect Sonny Chan. One of them, it transpires, is an outside cloakroom at one end of a lotus pool.

A thatched pavilion appears to float above the blue tiled pool (*top left*), while a pair of ornamental stone pigs spout water into it – in deference to Hindu mythology, Wijaya says. The pigs look on to a nature reserve, through Java palms (*Rhopaloblaste singaporensis*), so Wijaya designed a pool with a waterfall edge that follows the natural contours.

Behind the "Majapahit temple" (on the wall of which is carved a Java-style panel painted in yellow and blue), the planting of torch gingers over the pool is so thick that you don't see the water (*below*). The adjacent mass of heliconias looks as if it will eventually hide next door's wall. Meanwhile the white spider lily (*Hymenocallis littoralis*) struggles for the limelight (*bottom centre*).

Remembering that Vladimir Sitta's garden designs are naturally theatrical, in the best sense, I was expecting to find something different at Garangula, an 1850s' homestead in the wilds of New South Wales, in Australia. I was not to be disappointed.

The garden contains several exotic ideas but none quite so dramatic as the stone cone, with a split in it. It is made of rough granite and "hairs" of twisted copper rods around its top (*top right*), forming an eccentric crown. The copper used to be polished so that the tips reflected the sunset; however, this is no longer done.

Because the cone is positioned next to the swimming pool, Sitta had the idea of cutting a black stream, or Black River (Black River Farm being the original name of the estate), into the paving between the two. It took Sitta a day to draw its course on the floor of the factory.

The end result looks fantastic on site. The peak moment is when, at the press of a button, jets in the cone emit a fog of water vapour (*bottom right*), filling it very quickly. Gradually the fog then drifts out into the garden (*left*). It is known, naturally, as the "fog folly".

"So full of shapes is fancy that it alone is high fantastical", wrote William Shakespeare in *Twelfth Night*. The romance of peeping through into the as-yet-unseen is also fanciful.

Far left: Passers-by can enjoy a vista of this garden in New Jersey, USA, by looking through the fence. Richard Hartlage designed the window frame, put it in place, and painted it the darkest blue of the garden's three blue-coloured walls. He then softened the effect by planting *Anemone × hybrida* var. *japonica* 'Pamina' outside.

Centre: This is one of five arches set in a row within a wall of ivy-clad wire mesh with five mosaic-mirrored panels, all designed by Andrea Cochran. She created these mirrored arches to make the garden seem bigger and brighter. Her client in San Francisco, USA, had wanted Cochran visually to enlarge the 4.5 × 11.3m (15 × 37ft) garden space opposite the living room as well as to give it a 17th-century French look with a contemporary "twist".

Right: "Vertumnus", a 1590 portrait of the Emperor Rudolph II in the form of fruits, flowers, and vegetables, by Guiseppe Arcimboldo was the inspiration behind this mural in a walled potager in Buckinghamshire, UK. It was painted in situ, in shades of grey, during an eight-week period in autumn 1996 by the artist Owen Turville, who had been commissioned by Lord and Lady Carrington.

When Made Wijaya was asked by Shirin Paul to create a secret fantasy garden in the Lutyens district of New Delhi, India, he decided to adopt a mosaic theme, for example under the steps to the meditation platform (*right*).

With his Balinese team, Wijaya also began to build a mosaic pool whose water flows under a bridge (*far left*) and through to a grotto. Paul's architect daughter Priti, with Mexican inspiration, conceived the idea of decorating the bridge, the pool, and a water slide (*top centre*) in differing shades and patterns of blue mosaic and mirrors. In this, she was assisted by Raj, a local craftsman. The shape of the bridge, with its reflection, resembles a giant mouth at the entrance to the grotto.

Thrilled by success, Wijaya's team then built a red "Delhi-brick" gate as a folly (*bottom centre*), and Priti continued her wonderfully fluid mosaic. The circles, she says, are intended to direct footsteps to the door.

The garden also has a "tea lawn" on one side, boasting all kinds of vivid annual flowers grouped in clay pots at intervals on the lawn. They line stone paths and terraces and form a group of dahlias, verbena, phlox, nasturtiums, and petunias under the tiled staircase.

When I first visited the Eden Project in Cornwall, UK, in 2000, the biomes were still being fitted with hexagonal plastic panels and it was empty of any vegetation. What a stunning transformation eight months later: the Humid Tropics biome had been filled with plants and trees, which were all looking happy, at 35°C (95°F), as if they belonged there. The plants seemed unaffected by the 3,000 visitors a day to this "Eighth Wonder of the World".

The Dutch visionary responsible for conjuring up such an inspiring garden from an abandoned china clay quarry was Tim Smit, who had already pioneered the restoration of the Lost Gardens at Heligan, also in Cornwall. When looking back on events, Smit's philosophy is "I'm glad I did" rather than "I wish I had", having created an emotive, living environment within accessible grandeur.

High up in the West African section (*far left*), vines prepare the view towards the quarry cliff, while in the Amazonia section (*above*) pads of Santa Cruz water lily (*Victoria cruziana*) steal the limelight from the wealth of larger-leaved plants. The tropical islands/Malaysia section (*left*) contains a 30m (100ft) high waterfall, which rushes past the red-barked sealing-wax palm and the lance-like leaves of palm grass (*Curculigo cupitulata*).

Interpretations of naturalism in the garden vary. In the mid-18th century, for example, Henry Hoare thought in a naturalistic way when he planted vast areas of beech woods at Stourhead, in Wiltshire. Garden historian Patrick Chassé, among other contemporary garden designers, has continued this tradition in following his long-term vision to create woodland gardens in New England.

A naturalistic form of perennial planting surfaced in Germany in the 1930s under the influence of Karl Foersler who, later, taught Wolfgang Oehme. This style was further developed by Oehme and James van Sweden, who began the New American Garden in the late 1970s, using perennials in single bands of colour relieved by, the then, revolutionary idea of swathes of grasses. In time the naturalistic concept of prairie gardening spread internationally. The garden designer Keith Wiley believes that "a garden that has its origins in the natural landscape should look natural at any time of the year." That sentiment would meet with the approval of most "natural" gardeners, including Piet Oudolf and Ulf Nordfjell, especially when winter frosts or snow decorate sculptural stems.

the new naturalism

Previous pages: Keith Wiley planted his Cretan Cottage Garden, at The Garden House, Buckland Monachorum, UK, specifically with this view of St Andrew's Church and the hills of Devon and Cornwall in mind.

In the mid-18th century, a more naturalistic style of gardening gradually replaced the formal designs of André Le Nôtre. At Stourhead, in Wiltshire, UK, for example, Henry Hoare II, with the help of architect Henry Flitcroft, created some memorable garden vistas of a natural landscape.

These become apparent after a winding walk through the woods, away from the house.

The village entrance view of the stone bridge and the Pantheon, surrounded by beech woods, is the classic one (*left*): the more enclosed vista (*below*) is revealed from the Temple of Apollo, higher up in the woods.

Exotic broad-leaved trees have been added to the beeches by generations of Hoares. They also planted rhododendrons and conifers, and these have become an integral part of Stourhead's success as a much-loved garden.

To ensure that stretches of water look natural, their shapes should be appropriate to the surrounding fields and the horizon. Trees or wild flowers planted in the immediate setting will also help enhance the effect.
Below: While famous 18th-century designers such as "Capability" Brown and Charles Bridgeman were honing their reputations, there was one man who, after losing his job as Chancellor of the Exchequer, devoted the rest of his life to creating a water garden in the wooded gorge at Studley Royal, Yorkshire, UK. To do this, John Aislabie used the river Skell, which ran through his property. He designed a formal water garden with a pleasing simple series of moon- and crescent-shaped pools. Close-cut lawns appear to flow around them, and the Temple of Piety and surrounding trees are reflected in the water.

Right: One of the great landscape architects of the 20th century was the late Dan Kiley, who greatly admired André Le Nôtre's use of space. This is evident in the Kimmel garden in Connecticut, USA. There, even the meadow planting, seen from the formal terrace of the house, was part of the progression to the lake, designed to fit into the New England landscape.

William Robinson, the Irish gardening revolutionary, published *The Wild Garden* at the age of 32, and thus exhibited a distaste for formal gardening in the form of bedding, pleached limes, and any kind of topiary. He experimented with plants at Gravetye Manor in West Sussex, UK, which he bought when he was aged 47.

Robinson particularly enjoyed plants spilling over walls, growing into each other, mixed in a cottage-garden, naturalistic way. Self-seeding was his special pleasure, especially when Iceland poppies and forget-me-nots appeared through iris rhizomes (*right*). He also pioneered the attractive idea of encouraging red valerian to seed in stone crevices.

In addition, Robinson planted thousands of bulbs in fields surrounding Gravetye Manor and on the slope above the house, inspiring the new concept of "the spring garden".

Nearer the house he allowed more formality. It was here that Peter Herbert, when restoring the garden during his ownership of the Gravetye Manor Hotel, ensured the preservation of the wisteria and rose pergolas (*left*) as well as plantings en masse of, for example, catmint (*Nepeta* 'Six Hills Giant'), pineapple broom (*Cytisus battandieri*), and *Iris pallida*.

The naturalistic planting ideals of Wolfgang Oehme and James van Sweden are similar to those of William Robinson (*see p.151*). In 1978, they established the New American Garden style – the cultivated meadow that reflects the natural American landscape and frees plants from forced and artificial forms.

Oehme had studied with Karl Foerster, the German horticulturist and pioneer in the use of grasses in the garden, and van Sweden was a successful architect when they formed the partnership OvS. They went on to develop their quintessential reputation for large-scale gardens featuring huge drifts of perennials and grasses.

Up in the north of New York State, USA, OvS were asked to make a garden in a shaded woodland area. By a rocky path, they planted a vast spread of golden groundsel (*Ligularia dentata* 'Desdemona'), with ferns (*Dryopteris erythrosora*) and red grass plumes of *Miscanthus sinensis* 'Rotsilber' growing up on the rocky hillside, behind the owner's birdhouse (*right*). All this I came across in early morning autumn mist on what was probably one of only two or three times in the year when conditions are absolutely perfect for photography.

Three satisfactory variations on the natural gardening approach are demonstrated here in the American Midwest and England. *Left:* Prairie gardens of recent years, such as in Neil Diboll's garden in Wisconsin, USA, have been inspired by memories of tall-grass prairies stretching across northernmost USA and Canada. Diboll therefore filled his back garden with purple coneflowers (*Echinacea purpurea*) and golden rod. *Below:* Inspired by Beth Chatto's naturalistic style of gardening, Lady Cholmondeley cries, "It's difficult not to overplant, isn't it?" In her water garden at Cholmondeley Castle, in Cheshire, UK, the autumnal groups of waterside perennials include yellow-leaved hostas, royal ferns, and the mottled red disc-like leaves of *Darmera peltata*. For trees and shrubs, the star performers are the orange-leaved Japanese cherries and the bronzed branches of rocket-shaped *Taxodium distichum*. *Right:* Mirabel Osler's book *A Gentle Plea for Chaos* was just that. She and her late husband lovingly gardened in this naturalistic way on a hillside in Shropshire, UK, with paths mown in long grass and tall tulips growing under trees in the orchard. The pond, by what had been a pigsty, was strewn with *Rosa* 'Zephirine Drouhin', which brought "a recurring intensity of pleasure". The whole yard was dense with beautiful irises, ferns, candelabra primulas, mimulus, lady's mantle, and campanulas.

Judy Pearce has been geatly influenced by John Brookes and is a friend of Keith Wiley. Consequently her prairie garden (good from late summer until late winter) and steppe (mid-summer to winter) have caught more attention than her formal garden.

Pearce's planting adviser for this mainly plantsman's garden at Lady Farm, near Bristol, UK, is lecturer Mary Payne, who says that the way to make this kind of garden work is to watch how the plants react not only to how you treat them but also to the other plants. If they like it, plants will self-seed and look wonderful. Care should also be taken about how plants look together.

In mid-autumn, the grasses (*top left*) in the prairie catch the evening sunlight, particularly *Calamagrostis × acutiflora* 'Karl Foerster' and *Miscanthus malapartus*. Down by the stream (*centre*), a close-up of *Miscanthus transmorrisonensis* stands out against more grasses on the prairie. The candelabra silhouettes of *Verbascum olympicum* (*bottom left*) in the steppe suggest stability against the windblown shapes of the Mexican feather grass *Stipa tenuissima*.

Beside the fountain pool, the plant combination of autumn-leaved *Crocosmia* 'Lucifer' rising above yellow *Rudbeckia fulgida* var. *deamii* towards the striped *Miscanthus sinensis* 'Strictus' was excellent. The vista carried on to the dark red foliage of *Viburnum plicatum* f. *tomentosum* 'Mariesii' and *Prunus spinosa* 'Purpurea', as well as yellow-leaved *Cornus alba* 'Aurea' and, as a full stop, the pampas grass *Cortaderia selloana* 'Aureolineata' (*above*).

In southern Sweden, in a climate similar to northern England, landscape architect Ulf Nordfjell has created a spectacular naturalistic garden at Farstorp. In 2000, he was commissioned to move his show garden at the Gothenburg garden festival right into Farstorp. There was, however, the matter of appropriate scale to consider – the Farstorp grounds being extensive – as well as the need for the various elements to merge into the surrounding woodland. Nordfjell also had to make provision for the strong winds there and ensure continued shelter in this huge area after he had cut down more than 50 trees near the house.

After months of felling trees, a large pool was dug. An L-shaped path of cedar decking (*left*) now leads triumphantly over the water towards the remaining woods. Seen from under the arbour, early sun filters on to swathes of purple *Salvia nemorosa* 'Caradonna' backed by deschampsia grasses and tall feathers of miscanthus – a truly successful transposition from the exhibition garden.

When Ulf Nordfjell introduced his style of naturalism at Farstorp, in southern Sweden, he and the owners wanted to make this part of the estate more intimate, so they decided to increase the number of gardenside windows in the house and to make a water garden immediately below it. This was designed and built around a large rectangular pond, complete with a pebble beach, an arbour, and decking.

The high quality of the building materials (cedar wood, greyed teak, granite, and steel) is complemented by a large number of plants. This is unusual in Sweden, which experiences some extreme weather conditions.

Already, Chinese wisterias on six cedar pillars, water lilies, and grasses interspersed with perennial flowers, such as *Iris ensata* and *Astrantia major* 'Claret', give a beautifully mature, even poetic impression (*bottom right*). A white "wall" of *Artemisia lactiflora* Guizhou Group stretches behind the arbour and wisteria pillars.

The arc of granite stepping stones (*left*), curving away from the decked path between hostas on the left and *Butomus umbellatus* on the right, is typical of Nordfjell's philosophy on using different materials and plants in a naturalistic setting.

Elsewhere, silver *Artemisia ludoviciana*, salvias, and achillea surround a granite sculpture (*top centre*), and, in the woodland, white anemones rise through a mist of *Deschampsia cespitosa* 'Goldschleier' (*top right*).

The strongest design influence on Christopher Bradley-Hole, who designed both of these gardens, comes from Ben Nicholson. In the 1920s, Nicholson painted abstract canvasses in the Cubist style in panels of flat colour and, ten years later, after meeting Piet Mondrian, Nicholson went on to make three-dimensional reliefs. "This", says Bradley-Hole, "is what my gardenmaking is about – a sense of place through abstract geometry."

Left: Bradley-Hole was commissioned by John Coke to create a garden, at Bury Court, near Bentley, Surrey, UK, which would connect the house to the surrounding fields by combining formality and naturalism.

Bradley-Hole therefore planted a dream-like meadow with oversized grasses set within a tight, grid-like design. The grid forms a series of 4.5m (13½ft) square beds, with squares offset within each one. From them, grasses like *Miscanthus sinensis* 'Hermann Mussel' and *Molinia caerulea* subsp. *arundinacea* 'Skyracer' tower above perennials such as *Sanguisorba canadensis* and *Macleaya microcarpa* 'Spetchley Ruby' (*right*).

He also designed a pavilion as two cubes, with one cube offset and raised to seat height to form a bench on two sides. Being set within the beds and reflected in the pool, it creates a calm focus.

Below: At Lambourn, in Berkshire, UK, Bradley-Hole created a country garden with children in mind. Here he allowed the landscape to define the house and made a massive deck with shallow steps down into the garden, thus borrowing the 18th-century idea of "calling in" the landscape.

One part of this 0.25ha (½ acre) garden at Agnäs, in northern Sweden, has a certain "designed" look. Close perennial plantings, soft colours, and shapes surround a brick-edged lawn and a living space. A surprise, however, comes a few paces beyond where, via a narrow path, a long series of stone steps curve under birch and cherry trees down a 45-degree hillside to a fast-flowing river. The River Ore meanders through pine-wooded slopes and banks of sand, the stream whooshing over the rocks to a landscape of small islands and hills.

This most delightful, naturalistic part of the garden was created by Ulf Nordfjell and Leif Haggkvest. On a wide, steep slope, mass plantings of different perennials appear to flow down to the river (*left*). Yellow *Iris pseudacorus* are near the tall cranesbill *Geranium phaeum* 'Samobor' and farther along are the white stars of *Gillenia trifoliata*. Below them grow red-spiked *Heuchera sanguinea* 'Splendens'. The blue spread is of *Polemonium caeruleum* 'Heavenly Habit', with yellow day lilies (*Hemerocallis lilioasphodelus*) peeping through and the catmint *Nepeta racemosa* 'Walker's Low' stretching over to the right.

Moss gardening, begun as far back as the 8th century in Japan, has sensuous delights extending beyond the visual. They include the soft, ripply feel of walking on moss barefoot.

Left: One afternoon at Saiho-ji in Kyoto, Japan, the Moss Temple Garden was full of atmosphere, with maples just approaching peak autumn colour. This lakeside area had been reconstructed as a stroll garden in 1339 by the priest Muso Kokushi, and it is now carpeted by more than 40 varieties of moss. I was by myself in the quiet atmosphere, where the moss helped to deaden sounds from over the wall, encouraging contemplation.

Top right: Jeff Mendoza has created many Kyoto-inspired Manhattan gardens, where the idea of a secluded space several floors up is not only appealing but also desirable. In this naturalistic roof-garden in New York, USA, the carpet of Irish moss (*Minuartia verna*) is a soothing counterpoint to other plant textures such as that of the hay-scented fern *Dennstaedtia punctilobula*, which is shaded by delicate-leaved *Acer palmatum dissectum* 'Viridis'.

Bottom right: In 1980 the landscape architects Richard Haag were hired to begin the moss garden at the Bloedel Reserve, on Bainbridge Island, Washington State, USA. The area is now covered with moss and strewn with moss-coated trees and stumps. True moss growth is encouraged by covering the stumps first with Irish moss, which after a year is naturally supplanted by "true mosses" such as *Eurhynchium praelongum* and *Brachythecium frigidum*. In turn, these both disappear to make way for more vigorous *Rhytidiadelphus loreus*.

Garden historian Patrick Chassé has developed an eclectic style of new naturalism. In this, he has been influenced by the work of Beatrix Farrand, who was the first American woman landscape architect.

On a damp autumnal day, Chassé took me to the White garden in Lewisboro, New York, USA. Each of the gardens immediately around the elegant Classical Revival house is classically inspired, including a labyrinth, a theatre court, a pergola, and a grotto. The garden extends into the indigenous forest, where Arcadian images are allowed to coincide with the New World flora.

Below the terrace, a path leads past Chassé's vivid display of autumn colour into the forest. Maroon-tinted branches of *Acer palmatum* f. *atropurpureum* overhang red and orange mounds of cut-leaf maples (*A.p.* var. *dissectum*), while the yellow leaves of the spice bush (*Lindera benzoin*) show up well (*below*).

The newest area is hidden in the forest along a natural brook. It is there that Chassé – an expert on mosses – has designed an Asian-inspired moss garden, which is covered in leaves (*right*).

Patrick Chassé first began work on Ed and Vivian Merrin's naturalistic garden in New York State, USA, in 1987. Among other highlights, he devised a glorious view of the private lake from the house, seen here through autumn leaves of *Magnolia* 'Elizabeth' with a red oak hanging lower (*left*).

Chassé designed the "crow's nest" as a lookout over the lake (*bottom centre*). It has a wall of rounded, 12.5cm (½in) thick glass, and the design for its stone platform was taken from a Japanese millstone. The whole structure is fixed to the top of an iron column – partly obscured here by red-leaved euonymus.

Across the garden, a man-made pond, near the natural lake, presented Chassé with an opportunity for ornament not allowed on natural lake shores. A pavilion is cantilevered above the pond edge, festooned in wistaria. It overlooks a zigzag plank bridge (*top left*), which, in summer, is surrounded by lotuses and water lilies. A marble gargoyle (*bottom left*) spouts water into the pond on the far side.

A curving drive or a winding path through single-plant schemes can be just as effective as combining different plants of the same colour in their own space.

Left: Lemon-scented gums (*Eucalyptus citriodora*) dominate the drive at Cruden Farm in Victoria, Australia. They were planted in a long curve in 1933 by Keith and Elisabeth Murdoch and are now more than 45m (150ft) tall. Dame Elisabeth Murdoch extended her naturalistic thinking by creating and planting a lake at the end of the 1980s. It is now home to large numbers of birds.

Centre: Jacqueline van der Kloet has been influenced by Gertrude Jekyll and, more recently, by Neil Diboll's prairie gardens. She is always looking for new inspiration for her simple style of planting. Here in her garden at Weesp in the Netherlands, the white peony *Paeonia lactiflora* 'Duchesse de Nemours' is at its peak among the leaves of *Kirengeshoma palmata*, along with the small white flowers of *Anemone canadensis*.

Far right: The woodland at Iford Manor, in Wiltshire, UK, is threaded with a winding path through a carpet of another white-flowered plant – the more invasive wild garlic (*Allium ursinum*). As your feet brush the path edges, you inhale the distinctive smell of this specially planted herb. Such a naturally wooded area needs little or no maintenance, unlike Harold Peto's Italianate part of the Iford Manor garden (*see p.33*).

"The future of the garden seems assured, as our young head gardener … is a hard worker, very observant, and has good taste." So wrote Lionel Fortescue of Keith Wiley at The Garden House, Buckland Monachorum, in Devon, UK, in 1981. He was not to know what a firebrand his gardener would become. Wiley uses full expression when speaking of his kind of gardening, which is of the wider countryside, of new naturalism.

The walled garden at Buckland Monachorum has double borders running between the tower and a thatched cottage (*bottom left*). Wiley's freedom of planting here included perennials such as *Campanula lactiflora*, pink *Sidalcea malviflora*, the blue monkshood *Aconitum* 'Bressingham Spire', and tall filipendulas.

A trip to Crete with his wife Ros to see wild orchids was "the catalyst and the coalescence" for Wiley's Cretan Cottage Garden, begun in 1979. Having seen the wild flowers in their native habitats, Wiley purposely made no controlled colour combinations or heights. Here, Californian poppies jostle with *Hosta sieboldiana* in the foreground (*right*), while heads of white wild carrot, yellow anthemis, grey-leaved *Lychnis coronaria*, and pink *Geranium palmatum* flourish behind.

More recently, Wiley found the ideal space for planting alpines, so he made the Quarry Garden (*top left*), which includes a stream and a rustic bridge. Here are purple and white creeping thyme, helianthemums, and grey-leaved *Dianthus* 'Brymos', backed by blue-flowered, silver-leaved *Lupinus versicolor*.

Wiley and his wife are currently setting up their own garden nearby: he has years ahead in which to disseminate his ideas still further.

The pretty village of Netherbury, set in the Dorset hills, in the UK, is where Simon and Amanda Mehigan have created a delightful garden at their Old Rectory home. It is very much in sympathy with the surrounding landscape and is the product of an ideal arrangement. Amanda Mehigan did the planning and design, while Simon Mehigan was in charge of the heavier, structural jobs.

A formal walk from the house, through an avenue of yew pyramids, leads to the bog garden, which until 1995 was a stand of overgrown dense pines planted by the previous owners. Once the area had been cleared by the Mehigans, the informal nature of the meandering stream in its midst encouraged them to create a natural planting scheme – the husband-and-wife team being admirers of both Beth Chatto and Keith Wiley.

Over the following three years, they established delicate, airy plants that create freshness and light in the bog garden, and they kept the larger bog plants such as rodgersias and gunneras to a minimum. The stream now runs through *Iris sibirica* 'Silver Edge' and *I. pseudacorus* var. *bastardii*, with *Hosta sieboldiana* in the foreground (*far left*). Typical of Amanda Mehigan's sensitive grouping of plants is that of the arum lily (*Zantedeschia aethiopica* 'Crowborough') with *Iris laevigata* and *Primula florindae* (*centre*).

The summerhouse (*below*) was positioned near the stream as a focal point among yellow *Iris pseudacorus*, blue *I. laevigata*, drifts of *Primula japonica* 'Postford White', *Hosta sieboldiana*, and, in the grass on the far bank, pink ragged robin.

The tithe barn at the Manor House, in Buckinghamshire, UK, was destroyed by fire in 1968, and this was chosen by Lord and Lady Carrington as the moment to start a new garden around the 300 year-old house. Ever keen to foster new talent, they engaged a young professional, Robert Adams, to design it.

Adams made several formal gardens before the Carringtons asked him to design the Lyde Garden, a naturalistic dell area around a stream called the Lyde. Adams channelled the stream into a series of pools and devised a raised deck to wind over and around the boggy water. The stepped path then led up to a bridge over the stream and through the trees, hundreds of which were planted in the dell.

Because the Lyde Garden is so well structured, I went to photograph it once the leaves had fallen. The day I arrived, in mid-winter, frost and fog hung on the trees and the boxwood sugar loaves (*below*). The 11th-century church rose high above the garden (*left*), and the deck stretched across the view.

I revisited in spring, when a small oriental aviary in the water was surrounded by willows, irises, and yellow *Primulae florindae* (*above*). The Lyde is paradisiacal and, apart from the birds singing, rather quiet.

In the 1930s, Karl Foerster encouraged a natural style of perennial planting, including the use of grasses, compatible with each other and local conditions. Piet Oudolf's garden for John Coke at Bury Court, in Surrey, UK, is a part of that thinking.

They had been friends for some time when Oudolf offered to help Coke plan his walled garden. Although Oudolf had designed little outside Holland at that time – the early 1990s –

Coke accepted. In his design for the walled garden, Oudolf sought not only to further naturalism in the garden context but also to show his design talents within an enclosed space.

The garden walls are a natural background for plants such as spiky eryngiums (*top centre*). The walls are of brick and stone, the lines of which are interrupted by the curved oast houses (*top right*), which had originally been used for drying hops.

In one curving bed (*above*), sweeps of *Echinacea purpurea*, with tall *Rudbeckia maxima* growing through them, enfold groups of panicum grass.

By another wall, red *Persicaria amplexicaulis* (*bottom centre*) fronts a bed containing blue spheres of *Echinops ritro* 'Veitch's Blue', tall *Helianthus* 'Lemon Queen', Joe Pye weed (*Eupatorium purpureum*), and, on the left, *Stipa gigantea* – one of the most showy grasses of all.

Two gardens close to the house in different climates illustrate how naturalism can be successfully incorporated into the living space.

Left: Eric Nagelman was commissioned to design a garden with an overgrown, natural look for a coastal property in California, USA. This was to fit in with the house, which had a rusted, corrugated-iron roof.

Despite the hot environment, coastal winds, and poor soil, in mid-spring Nagelman's garden includes banks of flourishing flowers such as red *Arctotis* 'Big Magenta' and purple *Pelargonium* 'Francis Grate', planted between lime-green mesquite tree and grey-leaved melaleuca. Behind them, five stems of spiky *Dyckia tuberosa* form a focal point from their metal planter.

Right: At the highest point of a Stockholm garden, in Sweden, Ulf Nordfjell designed a natural living and play area at the top of some rocks. It is reached by climbing either side of a rill, which flows down to the water garden. The rill is served by water pumped and recycled back to the top of the rocks.

The deck area is planted with irises and carex grasses, with red *Persicaria amplexicaulis* thriving under the fountain-like leaves of *Miscanthus sinensis*. *Calamagrostis* × *acutifolia* 'Karl Foerster' grows just above.

Tulips in their original habitat, the mountain valleys of Asia Minor and central Asia, grow in meadows, an environment that some gardeners enjoy trying to emulate.

Left: Hermannshof, in Weinheim, Germany, was the inspiration of Urs Walser, a man who loved the wildflower communities of the Alps and who applied his artistic flair and knowledge to creating a prairie-style garden. His retirement in 1998 made way for Cassian Schmidt, an enthusiastic plantsman who had tried his hand at landscape architecture.

In late spring, the Judas trees (*Cercis siliquastrum*) are thick with blossom among randomly planted tulips growing through perennials near the wisteria walk. In so large a garden, it is easy to forget that you are in the middle of a town.

Top right: Long stretches of Castle Mainau's island garden, in Germany, have been made to look naturalistic under the direction of the late Count Lennart Bernadotte. He planted a million tulips in the grass either side of an avenue of knotty sycamore and chestnut trees.

Bottom right: Flower-arranger George Smith's planting of the 'Apricot Parrot' tulip among tall *Nectaroscordum siculum* is in a more controlled style. This is on a sunny, sandy bank at The Manor House, Heslington, UK.

Exotic gardens are often strikingly unusual, faithful to the cultures and traditions of countries sometimes far away from where they are to be found. Frequently they are filled with exciting and very colourful plants. "The great thing about tropical plants in a temperate climate is that they are really theatrical", says American designer Richard Hartlage. "The scale of the foliage, the scale of the plants, and the rapid growth rate are things that everyone loves." While visiting gardens in tropical Brazil, Indonesia, and India I have also found gardens filled with exotic ideas from temperate regions. For example, I enjoyed the fact that Sir Edwin Lutyens had planted the beds of his Mughal-influenced viceroy's palace garden in New Delhi with colourful English annuals and that in California Isabelle C. Greene had recently designed a garden based on the stepped terraces of rice-paddy fields.

The best kind of exotic gardening influence is handed on, as between the plant collector and designer Roberto Burle Marx and the Miami landscape architect Raymond Jungles. Subtly, the technique and the thinking changes – and develops to reach yet more exciting levels.

the exotic look

Previous pages: Both Raymond and his wife Debra Yates, creator of brilliant tile murals, cooperated with Roberto Burle Marx on the Dunn town garden in Key West, USA. With the Jungles/Yates wall fountain as focal point, exotic plants such as Cabada palms (*Dypsis cabadae*), *Philodendron* 'Week's Hybrid', and *Cordyline fruticosa* 'Peter Buck' make up the foreground with *Allamanda cathartica* 'Cherries Jubilee' flowering above.

Roberto Burle Marx was fortunate to have been born in and to live in a huge and wonderful country – Brazil which was as exotic and larger than life as he was himself. As a young man he travelled in Europe in the 1930s, discovering its culture and artistic achievement. When he returned home, he joined the intellectuals who had ambitions for Brazil, its resources, and its exuberance.

Burle Marx found the Sitio, his home, his garden, and his nursery at Santo Antonio da Bica, near Rio de Janiero. Here, he collected plants including architectural ones such as the yellow-to-orange gingor *Zingiber spectabile* (*bottom centre*). He also created 0.6ha (1½ acres) of greenhouses and seedbeds in a garden of different levels separated by long, hilly slopes. These lead, via a paved road, to a 17th-century chapel dedicated to St Anthony, to the house … and to a concert hall, built later in Burle Marx's life.

Most of the garden space is under a forest of trees reaching skywards. It is filled with mass plantings ranging from desert plants such as big, spiky furcraeas to ground-cover ones such as liriope and ophiopogon. The exception is around the formal lawns and pools near the house, where bromeliads and palms grow in, around, and on top of stone pillars and walls (*above*). Bromeliads also thrive on a multipanelled, multicoloured structure designed by Burle Marx (*far left*). The frog (*Hyla albofrenata*) (*top centre*) was photographed under the jade wine pergola of the house, from which it makes tropical percussion music on rainy days.

Roberto Burle Marx often said that he made extraordinary gardens for many people but not for himself, even at the Sitio, which he regarded as an experimental area.

Some 30 years ago, Burle Marx led a plant-collecting expedition, which included the present director of the Sitio, Roberio Dias, and then went north to Bahia. With his northern finds, Burle Marx began planting the lower lake, which is quite secluded and is rich in rocks and huge trees.

Maroon-coloured leaves of *Colocasia esculenta* var. *aquatilis* (*right*) curve around the lake en masse to reach hanging stems of *Euphorbia phosphorea* and the lily pads of *Victoria amazonica*. Nearby is a green philodendron, while on the right the heart-shaped leaves of *Montrichardia linifera* stretch up high.

While the gardens of Roberto Burle Marx could always be described as exotic, the approach varied according to the location. The one which gave him the most satisfaction, and to which he was often going back with gifts of plants, was Fazenda Marambaia near Petroplis, Brazil. Here, in 1948, his vision was for a garden with long swathes of grass winding through the valley floor around a small lake that acted as a focal point (*top right*). Gravel paths would then lead to a rain forest. Trees were felled, except for more decorative ones such as the purple-flowering *Tibouchina mutabilis*. Flower beds now swirl around in irregular, single-colour shapes, while grey-leaved *Helichrysum petiolare* and the purple *Iresine herbstii* nestle together. A new area, created in 1992, involving a falling water design (*left*), was created with the assistance of Haruyoshi Ono. *Bottom right:* Burle Marx's talents as a painter extended to his distinctive designs for tiled walls. This curving version, created for Walter Moreira Salles' town garden in Rio de Janeiro, is quite exceptional, reflecting in the pool among orange-flowered heliconias and pennmisteum grasses.

Lotusland without the lotuses, in spring: Madame Ganna Walska, self-styled diva and "enemy of the average", as she called herself, might have seen the irony of this at Lotusland, her estate in Montecito, California, USA. She began the exotic "theatre" there in 1942 by filling what had been an old swimming pool with lotuses and renaming the estate accordingly.

Landscape architect Lockwood de Forest was the first to help reshape the garden. He began by surrounding the front and side of the house with truckloads of organ-pipe cacti (*top right*), including white-flowered *Echinopsis spachiana*), for visual effect.

When he left, Ralph Stevens advised Walska for many years and oversaw the creation of the shell beach. This included the Abalone Shell Pool designed by Joseph Knowles Sr, with fountains of giant clam shells (*bottom right*) mounted on columns of coral.

In 1948 Stevens began the Blue Garden (*below*) by ordering several Atlas cedars (*Cedrus atlantica* Glauca Group) and blue hesper palms (*Brahea armata*). These were planted in blue fescue grass (*Festuca glauca*). At the entrance, he grew *Agave americana* and *A. franzosinii*.

Visitors to Carol Valentine's unorthodox garden at Montecito, California, USA, are reminded of rice terraces in south-east Asia, sentiments with which its designer, Isabelle C. Greene, concurs. Greene, with her distaste for geometric lines, felt impelled to offset the house's svelte lines with a garden which could be described as its antithesis.

A side garden on house level has Japanese simplicity (*bottom centre*). Blue gravel represents water and beige gravel the mountain earth. The Japanese-inspired platforms hold sculptures and mottled spheres, sheltered by bougainvillea on the balcony wall. Around the corner is a varied collection of succulents (*bottom left*), including *Kalanchoe beharensis*, echeverias, and aeoniums.

In the main garden, wooden-moulded terrace walls are made of concrete and coloured in a warm hue (*right*). They sweep across the garden, falling into naturalistic, "moving" contours. The early morning sun picks up waves of plants (*top left*), including echeverias, blue anemones, grey *Lynchnis coronaria*, yellow zephyranthes, and 'Fragrant Apricot' roses.

Climbing *Rosa* 'Sutter's Gold', red in the Californian climate, blooms beyond the spiky Mexican grass plant (*Dasylirion longissimum*). Farther down again grow the lance-shaped, pink leaves of *Aloe vera* within a carpet of *Sedum rubrotinctum*.

As one of the most versatile modernist landscape architects, Mario Schjetnan is very much a Mexican/South American historian who is globally aware of 21st century art. In his weekend house, within easy reach of Mexico City, Mexico, he has put his design philosophy into practice by integrating indoor and outdoor spaces in a series of exotic gardens and unusual patios.

In late winter, we sat by a log fire in his open-to-the-courtyard house while Schjetnan reminisced about his friendship with Luis Barragán, who he believes to have been the complete aesthete, in a perpetual search for beauty. Yet the colours of Schjetnan's house wall were probably even more exotic than Barragán would have used. He has even added a colour-coordinated cactus – *Oreocereus doelzianus* (*far left*) – with its cerise flowers complementing the walls.

The pipe organ cactus *Stenocereus marginatus* leads visitors into the garden (*bottom centre*), along with agapanthus in a pot beneath a flowering bougainvillea. The garden is heavily planted but in a restrained way (*right*), with masses of comb ferns (*Nephrolepis exaltata*) in the beds and agaves (*A. attenuata* and *A. palmeri*) by the steps. Rising on the right, next to the house, is a papaya tree (*Carica papaya*) exotic against the pink and yellow house.

The reflecting pool with a rill running through the courtyard (*top centre*) is perfectly placed – an enviable piece of inspiration.

Penelope Hobhouse recalls
watching me in the extraordinary
Huntington Desert Garden in
San Marino, California, USA,
some years ago, strung around
with cameras. She remembers
thinking what a lonely life it is
to be a garden photographer –
which it sometimes is.

The impact of this garden is
startling because of the variety
of forms and shapes of the 4,000
plant species in a 4.8ha (12 acre)
garden, begun by William
Hertich in 1907. Gary Lyons, the
curator of the Desert Garden,
explains that the plants are
cared for "by doing very little".

The 80 year-old golden barrel
cacti (*Echinocactus grusonii*),
which come from Mexico, glow
in the evening sunlight (*right*),
while the silvery pincushion
cacti (*Mamillaria geminispina*),
just sparkle. The four species
of organ-pipe cacti behind are
natives in such countries as
Guatemala, Venezuela, Bolivia,
and Honduras.

Especially at dawn or sunset, truly exotic vistas are created by vast cacti, agaves, and sagebrush. These are all part of the natural scenery at Rancho Mirage, beneath the Santa Rosa Mountains in the Californian desert, USA.

Top centre: It was here that Steve Chase developed his design and planting ideas at his home and desert garden. He bisected a swimming pool with a narrow rill, and beside it placed four palms (*Trachycarpus fortunei*) in square planters. In a courtyard (*top right*), Chase planted tall, spiny, whip-like branches of ocotillo (*Fouquieria splendens*), which rise behind golden barrel cactus (*Echinocactus grusonii*). *Bottom right:* Chase also advised his neighbours, art collectors Theodore and Annette Lerner, on their house and garden. "This glorious site is the best kind of sculpture", remarked Chase. He and Annette Lerner worked on the garden together. I visited it in spring after a wet winter – hence the green hills (*above*).

Their choice of *Agave parrasana* next to blue-green cactus *Pachycereus pringlei*, with the saguaro cactus (*Carnegiea gigantea*) on the left, certainly complements the desert, the wildness of which "captured" the owners.

Meanwhile, *Cereus aethiops* grows through purple-flowered *Lantana camara* by the pool.

How often do you find a tropical jungle in suburbia? Expect the unexpected is a pretty good rule for life in general but especially in the world of garden design.

For his garden in the Manhattan suburb of Nutley in New Jersey, USA, Silas Mountsier wanted to break away from conventional open lawns, sometimes bordered with a spot of topiary or busy lizzies. After talking to local designers, Mountsier chose Richard Hartlage as his garden expert.

Hartlage realized that Mountsier was looking for a garden designed for walking in and contemplation, so he used his broad knowledge of plants to create just such a haven.

The garden, which is extensive for a suburban one, is entered through specimens of yew, ivy, and hostas, with a Yoshino cherry tree over the gate (*left*).

Near the house, Hartlage created a water garden with a round pond and masses of specimen plants, sometimes tender, that contrast strongly in scale, form, or texture. Here he also planted a single angel's trumpet tree (*Brugmansia* 'Milk and Honey'), the flower of which hangs like a lamp (*above*), with the prickly barked *Pachypodium lamerei* directly beneath.

The concentric pattern of granite squares makes the focal geometric point of the pool (*right*), which is backed by a hedge of the bamboo *Fargesia nitida*. Under the dark leaves of *Colocasia esculenta* 'Illustris', one of three low fountains bubbles up as a complement to the water lilies. The grass *Miscanthus sinensis* 'Silberfeder' and *Xanthosoma sagittifolium* 'Chartreuse Giant' enhance this restful scene.

These two extraordinary gardens exude a spirituality that makes them truly memorable.
Far left: The rock garden at the Ryo-anji Temple near Kyoto, Japan, is thought to have originated about 500 years ago, soon after the private estate became a Zen Buddhist temple. Each of 15 rocks is surrounded by small amounts of moss within an area of finely raked gravel. The raking suggests ripples around the rocks after they have fallen into calm water.

There are many theories about the symbolism of the design, but if any one garden in the world were to be the supreme setting for contemplation, it is the Ryo-anji, especially as here, at 7am.
Right: A man who appreciates its spirituality is Terry Welch, whose 9.7ha (24 acre) garden, at Woodinville, north of Seattle, USA, was part of the land of the Snoqualmie tribe for, he says, 10,000 years. His three quite different influences include the work of 18th-century British landscapers such as "Capability" Brown, Japanese philosophy, and his own Pacific north-west landscape. Welch's Zen garden, which is enclosed on only two sides, takes in the landscape, thus combining all three.

Nearer the house is Welch's bonsai collection (*top centre*). It is mainly of maples and was his original gardening achievement. Nearby, full-sized maples, pines, and *Rhododendron yakushimanum* flourish around a small pool (*bottom centre*).

The distinctive elements of the Japanese style are always recognizable, wherever they are. *Far left:* It is the Azumaya, with its classic Iromoya roof and peaceful siting in the ravine, which provides the Japanese touch at Les Quatre Vents garden, near Quebec, Canada. Here, autumn sun emboldens its silhouette with rusty coloured aruncus leaves in front. Frank Cabot had been inspired by his visit to the Sambo-in garden near Kyoto, Japan, in 1980. Ten years later, assisted by two Japanese super-craftsmen, this wonderful, spiritual garden had been completed.

Top centre: As Japanese gardens are much loved for their moods of peace and harmony, Professor Takuma Tono was commissioned to create just such a one in Portland, Oregon, USA, in 1963. The waterfall can be seen from the Stroll Garden through the red blossoms of *Camellia japonica* and the pink cherry tree *Prunus × yedoensis* 'Akebono', backed by another camellia.

Bottom centre: In reverse, the American designer Marc Peter Keane, while living in Kyoto, Japan, with his family, restored the garden of a samurai doctor. Keane cleared everything except for a Japanese maple *Acer palmatum* subsp. *amoenum*. He made it the focal point around which to plant a spiral of moss (*Pogonatum inflexum*). Keane covered the rest of the newly named Spiral Garden with fine white granite gravel, raked into a wave pattern. All it needed then was a border of scalloped roof tiles and black river pebbles.

Right: The 15th-century Taizo-in Temple in Kyoto, Japan, added a new garden in 1965, designed by Nakane Kinsaku. When seen from the bottom of the waterfall through a pine and a red maple, the sense of garden height is simply exhilarating.

Australian Michael White arrived on the shores of Bali more than 30 years ago as an architectural student and decided that he wanted to stay. Since then, he has developed his talents not only as an architect but also as an interior and landscape designer, changing his name to Made Wijaya along the way. *Bottom left:* Wijaya built the Villa Bebek complex of three villas and a cottage in Bali, in 1990. He was inspired by 1950s' Balinese

palace architecture – a blend of colonial and traditional styles.

In 1997, he pulled down the walls separating the villas and redesigned the gardens so that there are now 12 pavilions, including design studios, and 36 courtyard gardens, linking ponds, pergolas, and Balinese gateways. This is Wijaya's home, but it is also a hotbed of international design.

The garden and the pool are dominated by the water tower

(*top left*) with balcony rails painted aqua. In the middle of the courtyard, a coral-pink bougainvillea is trained up a frangipani tree so that it hangs like a parasol. Here also is flame of the forest (*Delonix regia*).

Wijaya set the red brick Balinese gate and sculptures among hurricane and Alexander palms (*Ptychosperma macarthurii* and *Archontophoenix alexandrae*) and, on the bottom of the pool, he painted wavy lines – a

reference to David Hockney's California pool paintings.

The Bali lamp (*top centre*) nestles among alpinias and long-leaved variegated pandanus, and is surrounded by water lilies. *Above:* In the water garden of the thatched restaurant at the Four Seasons in Jimbaran, Bali, Wijaya placed islands of springy palms and frangipani. Water plants encircling the islands include hyacinths, heart-shaped caladiums, and white water lilies.

The use of plants and structure in this Australian garden is very different from that in a New Zealand garden, yet both encompass aspects of exoticism. *Top left:* Peter Nixon's 22.5m (75ft) long garden at Paradisus, on the north shore of Sydney, NSW, Australia, boasts an extravagant variety of subtropical plants in all shapes, textures, and sizes, including a red and yellow, muppet-like plant called *Costus comosus* (*bottom left*). Intriguingly, the plants hide most of the main architectural feature in the garden – a mirror set within a wall fountain (*bottom centre*) at an angle facing down, so that when you do discover this feature it reflects back towards the house to show a new vista.

The work of Russell Page, who saw a garden as a refuge and for that reason combined his design with existing features, influenced Nixon when designing Paradisus. The front garden contains few clues as to what lies the other side of the rear deck, and here I can understand Nixon's reference to "refuge": the plant-filled space has a womb-like quality.

Above: A symbiotic synthesis of native and exotic horticulture has been achieved by Beverley McConnell and her late husband Malcolm in their Ayrlies garden, near Auckland, New Zealand. The garden contains ponds and streams on various levels and was inspired by Hampton Court, UK. In the lowest and quietest part of the garden, evening sun rim-lights a plume rush (*Restio tetraphyllus*) and yellow candelabras under a swamp cypress (*Taxodium distichum*), leaving white zantedeschias and Bowles' golden sedge in shade.

At the viceroy's palace garden in New Delhi, India, Sir Edwin Lutyens had the vision to mix English annuals, such as red *Salvia splendens* (*left*), with the water-garden ideas of the Great Mughals, imperial overlords of India who had dreamed of, and gone a long way towards realizing, paradise.

More than any other designer, Lutyens had been responsible for promoting the renaissance in British water gardening. In 1925, he received approval from the Indian government for the 5.5 ha (14 acre) garden of the palace, now the residence of the President of India, known as Rashtrapati Bhavan.

Lutyens ensured that his Mughal water gardens were not only "theatrical" in effect but were also sympathetic to the palace architecture. One way he did this was to include fountains whose jets of water rose high above tiers of 18-leaved sandstone lotuses.

The standard of horticulture in such a hostile climate is incredibly high at the Rashtrapati Bhavan garden of the President of India's palace in New Delhi. It evokes Coleridge's words about Xanadu and its "sinuous rills", written more than 100 years before Sir Edwin Lutyens created it in the early 20th century. The design of the rills, cascading to one of the intersecting canals, is based on the lotus flower in bud (*left*).

Soft curves and circles are recurring motifs in the Mughal garden: trees of *Mimusops elengi* are clipped into hemispherical domes, and the lotus leaves of the fountains are rounded.

A walk on wide, arrow-striped stone paths leads to a unique wall of sandstone hoops and one arch (*above*), which continues the circular theme. Through the hoops there is a grandstand view of the tennis courts, which it was meant to screen.

Farther on is a rose-covered pergola and the serene Round Pool Garden (*right*), which descends in tiers to the 18m (60ft) wide pool curbed in sandstone. Curving blocks of annual flowers repeat the main garden theme of grouping colour. They include white and pink stocks, yellow marigolds, red Sweet Williams, yellow pansies, red flax, and golden nemesia.

Exotic gardens filled with unfamiliar plants can happen where you least expect them. *Left:* The Abbey Gardens at Tresco in the Scilly Isles, UK, experience very little of England's habitual frost or rain because they lie 45km (28 miles) off the coast, on the Gulf Stream with its warming winds.

The Lighthouse Walk there leads up stone steps under tall *Phoenix canariensis* palms and giant *Yucca elephantipes* 'Variegata', past the spiky *Dasylirion acrotrichum* (from California and Mexico), right up to the bust of the sea-god Neptune. Curator Mike Nelhams remarks that the hotter, drier terraces at the top suit South African and Australian plants, while those below have the humidity for flora from New Zealand and South America. *Centre:* This beautiful slatted Palm House in a private garden in Andalucia, Spain, provides shade for sensitive plants as well as for those used to such conditions. The design was influenced by a similar structure in a park in Barcelona and built of iroko wood from South America. *Far right:* Marie Harley designed her terraced house garden in Stockwell, south London, UK, so that it possessed an exotic look. Friends from South Africa and Australia gave her wonderful aliens such as pink and red tea trees (*Leptospermum*), restios, red cordylines, and tree ferns (*Dicksonia antarctica*) to grow alongside a winding, river-shaped, gravel path. Harley completed the design by retaining her red *Paeonia officinalis* 'Rubra Plena' and deep pink *Rosa* Gertrude Jekyll.

It must be possible to design a satisfying garden without the flair of an artist to draw it all together, but it would be quite a challenge and would depend on the use to which the garden is to be put. Garden makers throughout history have known this, even if it has meant including just one piece of eye-catching art or sculpture.

One of many wonderful pieces of art in this chapter is the Palladian bridge at Stowe, in Buckinghamshire; other garden ornamentations reflect diverse contemporary ideas ranging from the conceptual to the spiritual to the devotedly modernist. There are also individual pieces of sculpture exemplifying the artist's own skill for making a focal point, without distracting attention from the garden. Each one is there to unify and decorate its surroundings as well as to stimulate the senses.

Many gardens themselves have been created as a whole work of art, in fine detail, from Naumkeag in Massachusetts, to Tony Heywood's streetside garden in London. They too are great standard bearers for artistic endeavour.

the garden as art

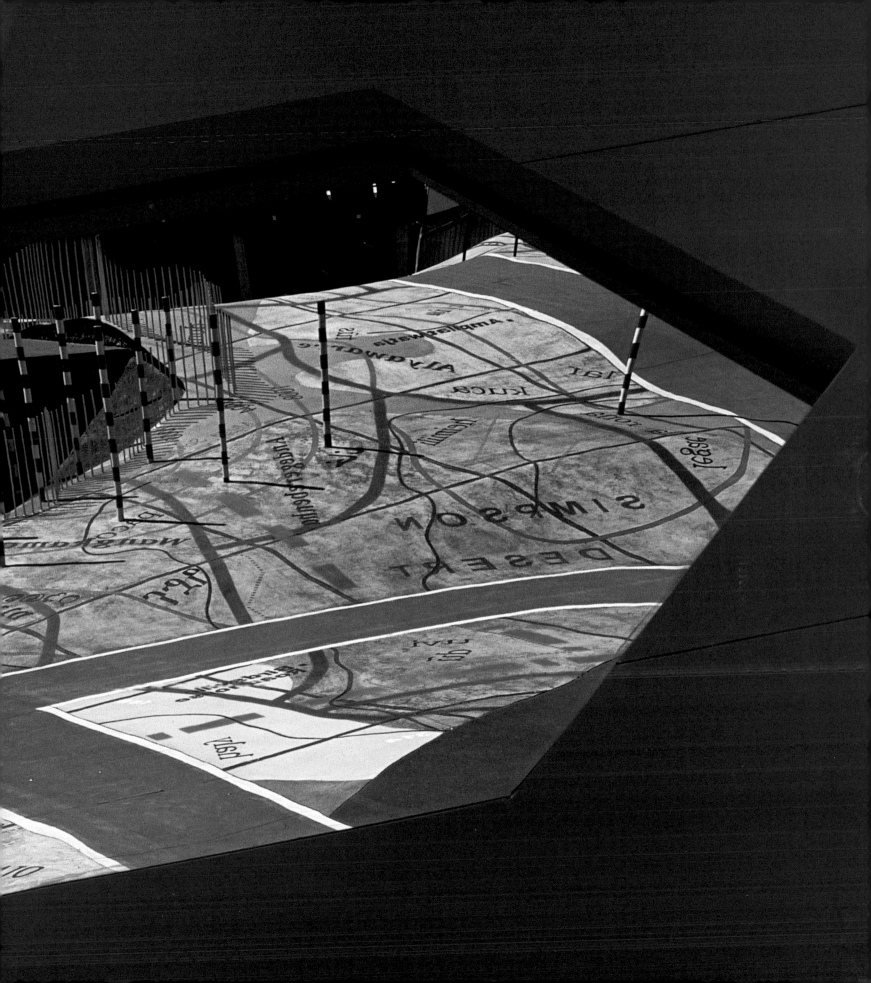

Previous pages: The Garden of Australian Dreams is here reflected in a window of the National Museum of Australia, at Canberra. This part of Vladimir Sitta and Richard Weller's collage includes the Simpson Desert in the heart of the country.

For 60 years, the meticulous Fletcher Steele saw gardens as works of art, and Dan Kiley thought him "the only good designer working through the 1920s and 1930s".

Steele's first creation for Mable Choate, the owner of Naumkeag in Stockbridge, Massachusetts, USA, was the Afternoon Garden, in 1926. This replicated the outdoor rooms she had seen in California and is now a shady water parterre. In 1933, Steele graded the South Lawn (*top left*), thereby adding the Oak Lawn and stressing the importance of swinging curves and slopes. Then, on the other side of the South Lawn, below the house, he based the curves of the rose garden parterre (*bottom left*) on those of the distant Bear Mountain.

The famous Blue Steps (*above*), begun in 1938, were constructed because Choate was afraid of slipping down the slope to her cutting garden. The idea of the curving handrails came from a visit to architect Clough Williams-Ellis's Plas Brondanw garden in Wales. Steele had six sets of rails made and painted them birch-tree white to reflect the birch trees he planted at different heights around the steps. He also decided to paint the step risers blue. Water for the concrete steps was supplied by a brick rill (*centre left*), bordered by mophead acacias.

The decision in 1967 of sculptor Richard Long to turn walking into an art form coincided with Sol de Witt's work on the basis of Conceptual Art. Long had realized that mere ideas can be works of art. "My work is visible or invisible", he says. "It can be an object or an idea equally shared by anyone of imagination." Thus his first creative walk was in a straight line in a grass field "going nowhere".

In 2001, Long was invited by Lady Bessborough to make a sculpture at Roche Court in Wiltshire, UK. For this he chose to set a long line of Norfolk flints along the slope of the land to an old ash tree (*below*). When it was nearing completion, Long noticed a buzzard watching the work, whereupon the sculpture was entitled "Tame Buzzard Line".

Long often uses the abstract shape of a circle, as here, where the semicircle comprises 10cm (4in) deep pieces of Cornish Delabole slate (*left*). The colour reflecting off the slates changes according to light and weather conditions. Created on the croquet lawn, with a view to the sea, he named it "Slate Atlantic".

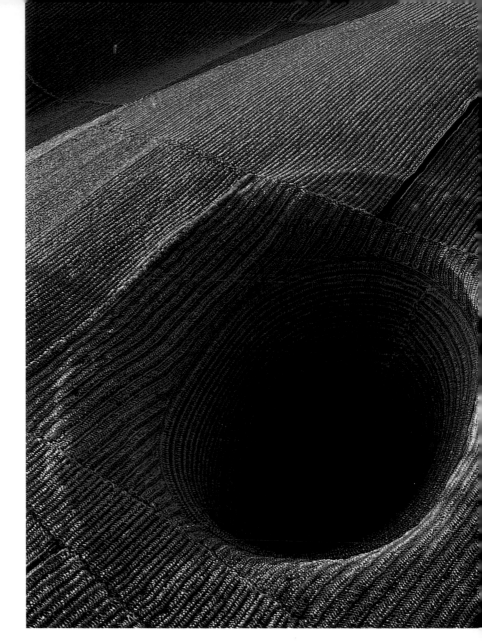

Andy Cao's brand of impressionism has much to do with reused and natural materials, some of which he introduced into garden design for the first time, in the mid-1990s. For example, his blue glass garden at Echo Park, in Los Angeles, USA, broke new ground and established his reputation for the unusual (*right*).

At the Chaumont-sur-Loire Garden Festival in France, Cao used 11km (7 miles) of Manila rope to ring the stage-like setting of his garden (*far left*), in which succulents such as *Crassula ovala* became vertical garden life.

In 2004, Cao collaborated with French designer Xavier Perrot – both being inspired by 19th-century Japanese woodblock prints. They travelled to Cao's native Vietnam for three months to direct 60 village weavers in creating 200 hand-knitted nylon carpets. These were later sewn together, on site, to make The Lullaby Garden at the Cornerstone Garden Festival, Sonoma, California, USA.

The carpet was draped over an artificial landform (*top centre*). Coconut shells were cut and polished for the entrance, and the shimmering fence was made from simple fishing line (*bottom centre*). The garden was infused with music, from Paris-based, Vietnamese musicians Huong Thanh and Nguyen Le, which emanated from the blue-lined vortex – music having partly inspired The Lullaby Garden.

In the town of Omi-Hachiman
in Shiga prefecture of Japan,
a famous 17th-century factory
produced clay tiles, known as
kawara. A competition to design
a kawara museum and a garden
on its site was won by the
iconoclastic and distinguished
architect Kan Izue, in 1994.

On the garden approach to the
museum, he laid paving tiles in
precise diamond and triangular
patterns (*right*). Reflecting the
museum's purpose, Izue chose
to use kawara tiles collected after
the 1995 Hanshin earthquake.

As they have a high rate of
water absorption, the tiles will
gradually harmonize with nature,
maturing attractively with moss
growing over them. The only
other planting in this garden is
of black bamboo (*Phyllostachys
nigra*) along the museum wall.

The mixture of natural materials and modern applications works best when used with imagination and some humour. *Left:* Having carefully positioned three standing stones in their wildflower meadow in Wethersfield, Essex, UK, Mike Springett and Jackie Tokley decided the view from their house was still not complete. Therefore, inspired by an article in the *Financial Times* about David Harber's Sundials, Tokley then purchasd a mirrored obelisk by Harber. She set it in the meadow among wild daisies and surrounded it by 12 stainless-steel markers. The obelisk is now a focal point, reflecting the standing stones. *Top right:* Ben Forgey, of New Mexico, created this driftwood cube on a stage "floating" above a meadow owned by James van Sweden (*see p.152*) on Chesapeake Bay, Maryland, USA. For it, Forgey gathered nearly 150 pieces of driftwood in New Mexico, with others from Chesapeake Bay.

The "folly" has two gates on each side, which when opened create four spires. This eye catcher is for sitting in, viewing the bay, and watching the ospreys raise their brood a short distance away. In light that appears green in photographs (*bottom right*), the gazebo glows at sunset. In the background, an osprey watches over its nest.

Stone and wood have been used as key elements in the design of these gardens.

Bottom left: In a garden in Sydney NSW, Australia, Vladimir Sitta's imaginative water course lines a stone path before finally leading to a front door. The rill flows into the pool, which crosses under the slate bridge. Sitta's exaggeration of irregular rhombic shapes of different tones adds to the dynamism within the garden.

Bottom centre: Steve Schubel designed this zigzag walkway to lead from the front garden around the house to a terrace that overlooks San Francisco Bay in California, USA.

The smooth teak boardwalk is suspended over a supposed "dry creek", and beside it are planted scented mock jasmine (*Trachelospermum jasminoides*) climbing on the house wall, ferns, and strong stands of the bamboo *Chimonobambusa quadrangularis*.

Right: This stone-dominated design was built by the German landscape architect Peter Latz for the Chaumont-sur-Loire Garden Festival in central France. He has softened the effect of the stones by feeding artificial fog through copper pipes breaking the soil surface – a popular device among contemporary designers keen to add something extra.

Despite the modernity of the installation, the fog in this early morning view of the garden appears to enhance the chateau, whose turrets are just visible.

The 1960s Water Gardens development on the corner of Edgware Road and Sussex Gardens in London, UK, boasts three gardens on different levels. Two of them – Helter Skelter (street level) and The Drop (on a roof terrace) – most typify the Conceptual Art theme. During the course of the two hours I was photographing there, passers-by consistently stopped to admire this exciting, living work of art.

It was created by Tony Heywood, whose self-driven graduation from head gardener to designer of Britain's most emotive characterization of this garden artform was supported by the owners of the gardens.

Heywood is fascinated by different textures, shapes, and materials. In The Drop garden, he created an ammonite-like stone spiral (*bottom right*) to represent a raindrop. It is surrounded by exotic plants.

In his Helter Skelter garden, Heywood impersonates the confusion of the streets, which border it. The stone, gravel, and moss influences of Kyoto are here, as well as his own passion to innovate. Ripples of dark grey slate merge into the moss, while large pieces rise end-on from a pool of blue glass chips (*left*) next to tussocks of blue grass (*Festuca glauca*). Curves of trained boxwood (*top right*) and polished stainless steel, with distorted reflections, jut out at odd angles. This is a garden for irresistible viewing, not for being in – there's no room.

Maureen Lunn's artistic inclinations are for variations of texture rather than colour, and these were gratified in the house built for her husband Larry and herself in Vancouver, Canada. It had been commissioned from Dan White, who became a friend.

The challenge for Maureen Lunn was to continue the textural theme in the garden, so she sought White's further advice. The Lunns and White travelled to a sandstone quarry in Seattle, because they liked the idea of their central sunken courtyard taking on a quarry theme. This proved to be impracticable, so, instead, great cuts of sandstone were brought up to Vancouver by truck to create a courtyard waterfall. This now cascades over a series of sandstone ledges (*far left*), shaded by maples and ferns, and culminates in a final 1.8m (6ft) drop into two reflecting pools by the house windows.

The house flooring continues in sandstone into the back garden. There, White designed a cantilevered table of polished granite (*below*) with a granite ball protruding through the top. Carved into the surrounding edge is a line from Andrew Marvell's poem "The Garden", Maureen being an inveterate poetry lover.

Originally, it was proposed to tumble some of the sandstones around the garden. However, the idea was eventually formalized (*centre*), as falling stones, the first two of which resemble a chaise longue. The stones are a magnet not only for wildlife but also as a climbing "frame" for children.

'Annihilating all that's made to a green thought in a green shade'

Andrea Palladio, the 16th-century Italian architect, said that "bridges should befit the spirit of the community by exhibiting commodiousness, firmness, and delight".
Right: The delight of the Palladian bridge at the Stowe Landscape Gardens, in Buckinghamshire, UK, comes from the sheer beauty and sensitivity of its design. Here it is on a late winter afternoon, crowned by the Gothic Temple. It was designed by James Gibbs in the 1740s and is thought to be an adaptation by Gibbs of the first English Palladian bridge, which had been designed by the Earl of Pembroke, the architect owner of Wilton House in Wiltshire, UK.
Top left: The original of Frank Cabot's Chinese Moon bridge at Les Quatre Vents in Quebec, Canada, is one of a pair of moon bridges, their arches 6m (20ft) in diameter, in the Chinese city of Giulin's Seven Star Park.
Top centre: Biddulph Grange, in Staffordshire, UK, survives from the age of Victorian gardening with picturesque effects, one of which includes a Chinese willow-pattern landscape, designed by James Bateman and E.W. Cooke. A zigzag fence leads to an ornate wooden bridge over a pool.
Bottom left: Totally original is Jim Partridge's "hedgehog" bridge at Olivers in Essex, UK. This is made of baulks of oak held by steel wire. Oak wedges force the baulks into an arc.

Naturalistic settings for different textures of sculpture materials work well when nature has made its own contribution to the work. *Left:* I found Rupert Till's wire netting sheep sculptures in a garden called An Cala on the Isle of Seil in Argyll, Scotland. The flock enlarges as and when the owner, Sheila Downie, commissions more.

As a medium, recycled chicken-wire netting is fairly malleable, provided it is only three or four years old and in good condition. On completion, the netting is regalvanized by dropping the sculpture into a vat of molten zinc at a temperature of 450°C (810°F), thus ensuring that, left outside, Till's animals last for a couple of generations. *Right:* Peter Randall-Page's "Three Fruit", in Lord Carrington's sculpture garden at Bledlow, in Buckinghamshire, UK, is a seminal work for him, having been his first sculpture of Kilkenny limestone. It was created in the mid 1980s. The fruit represents degrees of ripeness and fecundity. Randall-Page says that he wanted the forms to be full, almost to bursting, with the surface taut, like the meniscus on a drop of water.

Lord Carrington and I were standing under the beech tree beside "Three Fruit", with plumes of *Stipa gigantea* catching the morning sun above its curves, when he asked if I thought the lichen on the fruit surfaces should be removed. I replied, "No, it adds to the texture." On my next visit the lichen had gone.

Emerging from the railway station at Chandigarh, the Indian city designed by Le Corbusier, two things are immediately apparent: the chaos and the posters advertising the vast, extraordinary Rock Garden, where visitors are greeted by white mosaic geese standing on the garden wall (*top centre*).

Nek Chand, now over 80, worked secretly at night for 17 years to create his dream garden in a jungle clearing – his day job having been that of a roads inspector. Chand is now regarded as the greatest living folk artist, yet in 2004, with hundreds of people walking around his Rock Garden, I found him sitting unseen, watching the visitors go by. Chand told me modestly about the creation of regiments of sculpted men and women, immobile but colourful dancers (*bottom centre*), sportsmen, bears, monkeys, cattle, and birds made from urban debris. Stones were collected from the nearby hills on his bicycle and, by the same transport, he imported water in bamboo containers to water his plants. The expanding garden, however, contravened construction bylaws as well as the Le Corbusier plan.

Gradually, attitudes changed when the local council recognized Chand's unique and persistent talent and its potential spin-offs for the city. Water was made available, and in 1976 the garden was opened to the public.

Even without the photographs, my most abiding memory of this garden is of the cement mosaic figures which stand beneath the waterfall (*right*). However, the regimented monkeys perched on waves of tiles (*far left*), and watched over by exercising sportsmen and black-and-white giraffes, are like no other garden scene in the world.

Here are three individual artists with their own recognizable qualities, yet they are always producing different ideas.

Far left: Although Dale Chihuly studied interior design and architecture in the early 1960s, he had become absorbed by glassblowing by 1965. Two years later he was using neon, argon, and blown glass to create colourful, freestanding, plant-like sculptures such as "Cobalt-Blue Reeds". This sculpture is set by the lotus pool at Jack Lenor Larsen's LongHouse Reserve in East Hampton, on Long Island, USA, having been left as a gift after Chihuly's exhibition there in 2000.

Left: The use of water as a sculptural material is William Pye's distinctive talent, begun in boyhood when making dams and waterfalls in the stream at home. His is a continual quest for giving shape and form to water and ensuring that his structures work in a location sympathetic to his art. At Antony House in Cornwall, UK, water flows down the side of the tall cone, whose shape echoes yew topiary nearby.

Below: Surely, the globes in the Swiss Re Bank garden near Munich, Germany, have their origins in the formal pattern of bagels that Martha Schwartz made in her own garden, as a joke, more than 20 years ago. To counteract the shade from the bank's elevated buildings, Schwartz has used reflecting materials, such as glass, in areas inhospitable to plants.

When I asked the dynamic Topher Delaney who her influences were, she said, "the Russian painter Wassily Kandinsky" – no writers, composers, architects, or even landscape architects: just Kandinsky. I can understand that. Kandinsky's rainbow colours were applied with free, dynamic brush strokes, and Delaney has copied this style at the San Diego Children's Hospital in California, USA. She is an ex-cancer patient and has made gardens for several healing hospitals, identifying with the community.

Delaney wanted children to enjoy this garden from their first view of it, so she placed its entrance (*bottom centre*) between the legs of Sam the Dinosaur, which lights up at dusk. Sam is standing over "The Splash", which consists of concentric ellipses of concrete painted yellow, turquoise, and blue (*left*).

The walled garden is bounded by polychrome-curved walls, some of them overlapping and some punctuated with coloured glass discs and stars. Interior curved walls (*top right*) bear cutout shapes of exotic animals whose silhouettes are projected onto the ground by the sun. Nearby, the rainbow-coloured windmill (*bottom right*) gyrates to enliven the birds within. This is Conceptual Art as it should be.

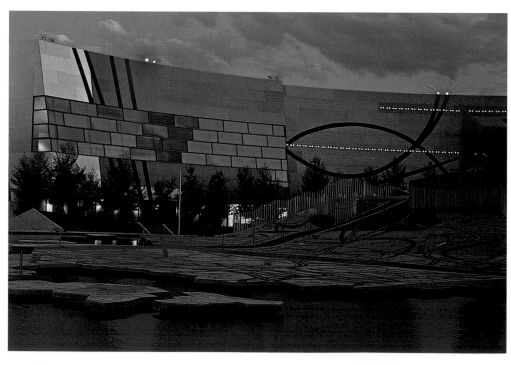

The Garden of Australian Dreams, at the National Museum of Australia in Canberra, is "a collage made up of history and culture" based on a map of Australia on and around which people can stroll, according to Vladimir Sitta, who collaborated with Richard Weller on its design. A prominent feature is the word "home" written in 120 languages, incorporated into the ground, where also are inscribed Aboriginal place names – the museum being dedicated to preserving the heritage and history of Australia.

Although there are trees, the garden is no verdant "dreamscape". It is, however, rich in iconography: for example, a Christian symbol is painted on the museum wall (*bottom left*). Reflected in the windows (*top left*) are two parts of the garden's Australian map, which relates to vegetation, geology, electoral boundaries, roads, and the history of exploration. Red-and-white striped poles atop a tunnel (*right*) symbolize the surveying of the land by the early settlers. The dingo fence, here represented in stainless steel, is in real life the world's longest continuous structure. It runs from the south Australian coast to the Queensland coast – just a few thousand kilometres of fencing to prevent these wild dogs moving eastwards.

"You can do whatever you like as long as it stays inside the box", Martha Schwartz was told when being commissioned to design a garden for Sam Davis and his wife Anne. In their plot in El Paso, Texas, USA, there are in fact six "boxes", all stuccoed and painted in vivid colours. They are perforated by small windows, which lead visually into the next box, or room (*top centre*).

Each room symbolizes a different aspect of the American scene, and in her treatment of them Schwartz acknowledges the influence of Luis Barragán (although André Le Nôtre and Roberto Burle Marx are also two of her heroes).

One room illustrates the barbed wire at the Mexican border with a grid of 22.5cm (9in) spikes jutting horizontally from one wall (*top right*). The effect on the imagination is bizarre.

An evenly sculpted mound of gravel in another room (*below*) brings to mind either the surrounding desert or the slag heaps of industry, while blue glass shards cresting some of the walls (*bottom right*) demonstrate America's current preoccupation with security.

The garden of Sam and Anne
Davis in El Paso is one of the
most important modernist
gardens of the 20th century.
It is certainly one of the most
innovative and is quite different
from anything else that the
brilliant Martha Schwartz has
made (even considering her roof-
top Splice Garden, plastic-based
and split diagonally with
Villandry on one side, Ryo-anji
on the other). Although some
people may believe that a garden
needs more plants in it to be
regarded so highly, Schwartz's
El Paso garden deserves its
reputation as a dynamically
structured work of modern art.

Within the garden, set below
30-year-old trees next to the
swimming pool, is a room with
red and orange walls (*right*).
It contains saguaro cactus
(*Carnegiea gigantea*) growing
proudly through a floor of pink
gravel. With its double (hidden
here), the cactus forms a focal
point for a series of square
windows in this memorably
artistic garden.

index

Jerry Harpur would like to thank the following:

First of all Jane Aspden who, as Managing Director of Mitchell Beazley, took on this project with some courage. The concept grew while most of the photography took place over three years.

Without the interest and co-operation of the garden designers and owners this book could not have happened and I am very grateful for their unfailing help and patience. However, there are several people, not named in the captions, who were instrumental in pointing me in the right directions and completing arrangements.

They include Tony & Annie Huntington, Dr Henri Carvallo, Claudia Ruspoli, Elizabeth Cartwright-Hignett, David Beaumont, Mark Brown, Hanako Yagi, Mary Armour, Anne Latreille, Lucy Tollemache, David Ward, Valentine Dillon, Daphne Charles, Drs. Tony and Lorraine Barrett ("Nooroo"), Myrna Ougland, Tania Compton, Karl Lauby NYBG, Marc Treib, Joyce Huisman, Mira Sadik, Federica Zanco, Colin Gunn & Sue Smith, Petronella Collins, Tim & Constance Stevens, Haruyoshi Ono and Isabela Ono, Mr & Mrs. Michael Earle, Sarah Blackburn, Richard Brown, Cassian Schmidt, Maria Regele, Dr. Roberio (sic) Dias, Catalina Corcuera, Marybeth Waterman, Cheryl Ching, Noel Kingsbury, The Indian High Commission in London, Mr S. M. Khan (Press Secretary to the President of India), Mike Nelhams, Robin Karson and Will Garrison, Helen Waters at Roche Court, Stephen Jerrom, Gay Edwards, Matko Tomicec, Dana Ragouzeos, Charles & Barbara Robinson and Cynthia & Chapin Nolen.

I value the professionalism of the team at Mitchell Beazley who have produced this wide-ranging book. Both Michèle Byam, commissioning editor, and Sarah Rock, executive art editor, have taken the eccentricities of this author in their stride and, in particular, Michèle has guided me skilfully through the ramifications of writing a book.

The distinctive design style was set by the wise engagement of Ken Wilson.

My wife Marjorie has borne the unpredictability of where I might be in any one week and my son and business partner Marcus has cleverly balanced my contribution to our garden photograph library. On completion of the text Joanna Chisholm made a brilliantly perceptive job of editing it, while Claire Bent-Marshall and Emma Levy handled many of the office technicalities of cyberspace.

Any compliment I pay to Penelope Hobhouse would be superfluous but I appreciate not only the honour of her writing the Foreword but also its balance.

I am constantly being inspired, not least by the enthusiasm of over seventy garden photographers in the UK alone. To everybody: thank you for helping my job, illustrated here, to be so totally compulsive.

author's
acknowledgments